S0-AKC-437

# How to Make One Million Dollars in Real Estate in Three Years Starting with No Cash

# How to Make One Million Dollars in Real Estate in Three Years Starting with No Cash

## TYLER G. HICKS

**PRENTICE-HALL, INC.**        Englewood Cliffs, N.J.

Prentice-Hall International, Inc., *London*
Prentice-Hall of Australia, Pty. Ltd. *Sydney*
Prentice-Hall of Canada, Ltd., *Toronto*
Prentice-Hall of India Private Ltd., *New Delhi*
Prentice-Hall of Japan, Inc., *Tokyo*

©1976 by

Prentice-Hall, Inc.
Englewood Cliffs, N.J.


*All rights reserved. No part of this book
may be reproduced in any form or by any
means, without permission in writing from
the publisher.*

Library of Congress Cataloging in Publication Data

Hicks, Tyler Gregory
    How to make one million dollars in real estate in
three years starting with no cash.

    Includes index.
    1.  Real estate investment.  I.  Title.
HD1379.H52        332.6'324          75-45048
ISBN 0-13-418491-2

Printed in the United States of America

## Also by the Author

*How to Make a Quick Fortune: New Ways to Build Wealth Fast*
*Magic Mind Secrets for Building Great Riches Fast*
*How to Borrow Your Way to a Great Fortune*
*How to Start Your Own Business on a Shoestring and Make Up to*
*    $100,000 a Year*
*Smart Money Shortcuts to Becoming Rich*
*How to Build a Second Income Fortune in Your Spare Time*

# WHAT THIS BOOK DOES FOR YOU

Every person in the world has two basic needs—food and shelter. There are thousands of firms supplying the food that we all need every day of our lives. Likewise, there are thousands of organizations supplying the shelter or real estate needs of individuals and firms of all kinds.

But of the two basic needs, the shelter need is probably served less efficiently. There are many reasons for this lower efficiency. *You* can help improve the efficiency of the shelter or real estate business and build great riches for yourself, using the magic power of borrowed money. This book shows you—step by step—exactly how to build enormous wealth in real estate ventures without investing a cent of your own.

Now what do we mean by shelter? In this book shelter means:

- Single-family homes
- Apartment houses
- Hotels and motels
- Factories
- Shopping centers
- Mobile homes
- Any other type of enclosure which provides protection for people and their possessions

Since every structure must be built on something, we'll also show you how to make enormous profits from borrowed money which you invest in:

- Vacant land
- Developed land

7

- Air rights
- Wetlands
- Offshore waters

Yes, there's a fortune waiting for every serious beginning real estate wealth builder who:

- Improves real estate
- Offers better values
- Pyramids his or her investments
- Takes "safe" risks

In this book I show *you* exactly

- Why real estate profits are so high
- Where to find *your* wealth-building properties
- How to borrow the money to build your real estate fortune
- When to buy, sell, rent, lease
- Which investments pay off best
- How scores of real-life people have built quick wealth in real estate

So—no matter what your background may be—inside or outside real estate—be you a:

- Beginner in property investments
- Experienced professional
- Real-estate salesman or saleswoman
- Doctor, lawyer, minister
- Bricklayer, plumber, plasterer
- Housewife, secretary, widow
- Worker in any field

this book can help you get richer—faster—in real estate, using the gigantic leverage of borrowed money. I have seen so many big fortunes built quickly in real estate of all types—from raw land to enormous residential-commercial complexes—that I'm completely convinced that you, too, can do the same, if you apply the methods given in this book.

For in the space of just a few short, fact-filled pages you'll learn how to:

- Get 100% financing for real estate
- Put together zero-cash deals

- Mortgage out—i.e. take over an income property, and walk away with cash
- Sell air rights over property
- Build enormous tax-free income
- Live free of charge in the best part of town
- Take over property for pennies
- Borrow your way to a real-estate fortune
- Build fast wealth using my proven methods

During my many years of helping others build their real estate wealth, I've met thousands of people who've used my methods successfully. I'll tell you about these people in this book. And I'll also tell you about my own real-estate deals, which are also successful money-makers.

So come along with me, interested real-estate wealth builder, to learn how *you* can get started on *your* riches program. I'm certain that you'll find our journey is interesting, challenging, and best of all, rewarding! Let's start—here and now.

Tyler G. Hicks

# CONTENTS

*11*

**How and Where to Get More Data on Real Estate** . 218

How to Make One Million Dollars
in Real Estate in Three Years
Starting with No Cash

# 1

# WHY REAL ESTATE IS FINANCIALLY VALUABLE TO YOU

Most of us live in houses, apartments, mobile homes, motels, or hotels for years without sensing the importance, from a money aspect, of the space we occupy. For if we live in a desirable area, the value of the shelter and space (land) we occupy is constantly rising. Time, as is proven again and again, is on the side of real estate. This means that time is on *your* side if you're a real estate owner.

## PRIME PROPERTIES PAY PROFITS

The law of the 4 Ps (which I developed) is at work 24 hours a day. This law is:

Prime Properties Pay Profits.
Also, prime properties increase in value, year by year.

And why do prime properties rise in value steadily, year after year? Because, some 70% of the population of the United States lives on about 2% of the land! This means that the 2% land area becomes more valuable as the population increases and larger numbers of people try to squeeze into a city or town of fixed area.

Further, the amount of land area available for real estate use rarely increases—if anything, this area decreases. And when you have more people—be they home owners, apartment dwellers, or factory owners—seeking a piece of a decreasing commodity (land or desirable shelter), the price of that commodity has nowhere to go but *up*! For this reason, land—and the shelter built on it—is one of the best investments you can ever make. Long experience shows that:

> The best investment made by the average person, from the standpoint of eventual profit, is in real estate. The profits the average person earns from real estate far outpace his or her profits in the stock market, antiques, paintings, and similar investments.

So you see, your chances of hitting the big money in real estate are much greater than in any other area of investment. And what's more important from a Beginning Wealth Builder's (BWB) standpoint is that:

> Real estate of all types is almost always financed with other people's money (OPM). So YOU ARE EXPECTED TO BORROW to buy real estate. Paying cash is the rare exception in real estate deals.

### KNOW THE IMPORTANCE OF SHELTER

Today we all take shelter for granted and expect:

- Warmth in winter
- Coolness in hot summers
- Dryness in fog and rain
- Protection from winds and snow
- Graciousness to improve the quality of our lives
- Safekeeping for our belongings

With inflation a fact of life since the invention of money, shelter which provides all—or most of—these features is constantly increasing in value—just like the land on which the shelter is built. It is the combination of these two value increases that will help *your* real estate investments make *you* rich!

## YOUR REAL ESTATE BUSINESS IS A SAFE BUSINESS

You can invest money in thousands of different businesses, such as:

- Manufacturing
- Services
- Leisure and sports
- Entertainment

and lose your shirt in a few months. But invest in well-located real estate and it is almost impossible to lose money. Why? Because:

> Well-located real estate is constantly increasing in value. There is almost nothing a sensible person can do that will permanently injure the value of well-located real estate.

So when I recommend real estate investments to you, I do so with the complete assurance that it is almost impossible for you to go wrong. Further, it is also almost impossible for you *not* to make money in real estate if you:

- Hold the property a few years
- Have the structures maintained properly
- Keep the property rented, if it is a rental holding

While it is true that real estate, like any other business, has its ups and downs, usually the swings are less severe than in other business—say retailing, like hardware, groceries, etc. So your real estate business is a safe business—and a business that can make *you* wealthy in a short time.

## YES—YOU CAN GET RICH FASTER!

Do you believe what I just said—"A business that can make *you* wealthy in a short time"? If you do not believe what I said, then—in this book—I hope to convince you by a series of real-life excerpts from letters that thousands of BWBs (Beginning Wealth Builders) have written to me telling me how they built their wealth using my methods—starting (in general) with no cash of their own. Each letter was sent to me voluntarily and is so valuable that I keep it in a safe deposit box. I'm sure you'll find these letters convincing, inspiring, and powerfully motivating to you.

In giving you excerpts from these letters, I'm following the practice I used in my six other money books, which are listed at the beginning of this book. What I did in each of those other books was to feature a special way *you* can get rich. And—I'm happy to say—I've made thousands of people rich—quickly, easily, and happily. Now let's turn to the first BWB who made it big in real estate. I call him the "From Debt to Millions" BWB. Here's his story, as given in his letter to me.

**From Debt to Millions**

> As I stated on the telephone, I was $12,500 in debt 24 months ago and have subsequently built a company with assets of approximately two million dollars. Prior to building the company I visited our local library and read many books. All the books offered some help. However, your book, *How to Borrow Your Way to a Great Fortune,* proved to furnish me with the ultimate plan. In this respect I owe you my deepest gratitude . . . . Again, I wish to thank you for everything you have done for me.

## KNOW THE ADVANTAGES OF REAL ESTATE

Real estate has many advantages for *every* investor—including yourself. These advantages include:

- Income-tax savings
- Capital growth
- Use of other people's money
- Multiple-loan financing
- Long life of property
- Constant rise in value
- Little management time required
- Zero-cash takeover of property *and* income

Let's take a quick look at each of these advantages to see how you can use them in your fortune-building program. You'll quickly learn how to get rich in real estate using borrowed money—that is, without putting up a penny of your own.

## SAVE ON YOUR INCOME TAXES

All shelter-type income-producing real estate—except vacant land—can be *depreciated. Depreciation is the money set aside from income to pay for the replacement of the structure, equipment, or other items for which rental, leasing, or other fees are received.*

Thus, let's say you take over a $100,000 income-producing structure which produces a $25,000 annual total income to you. Your operating expenses are $10,000 per year and your attorney tells you the structure has a life of 20 years. You and he decide that you will depreciate the building over 20 years on a *straight-line basis.* This means that you will deduct an equal amount each year during the life of the building for depreciation. So for this structure, you deduct $100,000 ÷ 20 years = $5,000 per year for depreciation.

In a given year, therefore, your total expenses will be $10,000 + $5,000 = $15,000. So you would pay taxes on $25,000 - $15,000 = $10,000 even though the $5,000 depreciation "expense" is money in your pocket.

If you use other methods of depreciation (sum of the digits, double declining balance, etc.) which are explained in low-cost Government books on taxes, you can save even more money on depreciation for the first 6 to 12 years in the life of the structure. Note here that land cannot, in general, be depreciated—just the structure and its equipment.

I know hundreds of real estate operators and they usually pay less in income taxes than any other business people. So you, too, can expect to pay lower income taxes on your real estate income than on almost any other kind of income. What's more, we'll show you how—when you have large real estate holdings—you can use your real estate depreciation to help you save income taxes on your other income.

## GROW RICH ON CAPITAL GROWTH

A dollar you put into income real estate today may grow this way:

| Year No. | Investment Value |
|----------|------------------|
| 1 | $1 |
| 2 | 1.07 |
| 3 | 1.14 |
| 4 | 1.22 |
| 5 | 1.31 |

Thus, in 5 years your $1.00 investment has grown to $1.31 while you:

- Are receiving income
- Are saving income taxes
- Are using OPM

So you see, capital growth *can* be an important factor in the increase of your fortune. Real estate is truly the magic business because:

> Real estate investments work for you 24 hours a day, seven days a week. So you can say that real estate makes money for you while you sleep!

## USE OTHER PEOPLE'S MONEY TO BUILD YOUR RICHES

Almost every real estate project you've ever seen is financed using other people's money (OPM) instead of your own. Very few real estate structures are ever bought or built using your own money. So if you—as a typical BWB—don't have much money to start building your fortune, you can go into real estate without worrying about borrowing the money you need.

Why should you—a BWB with plenty of original ideas—have to put up your own money? You shouldn't have to put up your own money if you're "putting up" the ideas. Plenty of banks, mortgage lenders, savings and loan associations, and other real estate financers are crying for good projects into which they can put the money which is overflowing their coffers.

Go into real estate if you want to:

- Build a fortune on OPM
- Borrow all the money you need with the greatest of ease
- Get more than one loan at the same time

### A Fortune for the Price of Manhattan Island

Another happy reader who has gained success using OPM in real estate recently wrote saying:

> It is with the greatest pleasure that I write to you and say *Thanks!* Nor am I forgetting Mr. Hicks who is kind enough to share his knowledge with the world. Four months ago I was

beating my brains out trying to make ends meet. Now just the reverse; I am beating my brains out trying to spend my money wisely.

It all started when I read Mr. Hicks' book, *How to Borrow Your Way to a Great Fortune.* I suppose I have read this book a dozen times, and still refer to it from time to time. After subscribing to *International Wealth Success* I was on my way. I followed Mr. Hicks' instruction to the letter, pyramiding loans, obtaining leads for second mortgages from IWS[1] and then purchased my first apartment house. I now own four and am in the process of buying a shopping center. Just think. All of that for twenty-four dollars! The same price as Manhattan Island.

## GET MULTIPLE-LOAN FINANCING

Many people think that having more than one loan at a time is somehow indecent. Yet, in real estate financing, multiple loans—that is more than one loan on a single piece of income property—are very common. Many income-producing properties routinely have two loans (mortgages) on them. Some properties have as many as eight mortgages (loans) on them!

So go where the money is—to the country of the multiple loan—the real estate income-property business. Earn big money using other people's money to finance still other people's property without investing a cent of your own! Get paid for your creative ideas and management ability.

Forget your fear and horror of the multiple loan. Instead, use multiple loans to finance your way to a real estate fortune!

### Three Days to Wealth

A happy reader using multiple loans writes:

I just got my loans. It took only three days to get $25,000. I pyramided five $5,000 property-improvement loans on a building I don't even own yet. I've taken over a $200,000 38-unit apartment building and borrowed the down payment. The cash flow pays all the loans too. By carefully timing the close of escrow, prorations of rents and payments, I walk away with $3,000 cash and a building for my trouble.

---

[1] The BWBs monthly newsletter of great wealth chances for you. To subscribe, send $24 for 12 monthly issues to IWS, Inc., Bank Plaza, Merrick, N.Y. 11566.

I'm looking at three more buildings that are even better. Every bank in town and some out of town ones too are trying to lay more cash on me than I can ever spend. _____ Bank and _____ Bank miniskirted PR girls are taking me to lunch offering lines of credit, compensating balances, ball-point pens, and blue-chip stamps.

I'm putting students and alcoholics to work as apartment managers, painters, carpet layers, plumbers, and giving senior citizens a good place to live and doing a lot of real good things. I'm thrilled and delighted. I have all of Ty Hicks' books, The *Starting Millionaire Program* and *Financial Broker Program.* [2] Many thanks for your ideas and assistance.

Note that this reader used three of my wealth-building methods, namely:

1. Get your money fast—it took just 3 days here
2. Use multiple loans—five here
3. Mortgage out—he got $3,000 more cash than he needed

You can learn how to do the same—if you keep reading this book.

## BUY LONG-LIFE PROPERTY

Buy the usual auto, TV or outfit of clothes and you'll wear it out in four years or less. Then you're faced with buying a replacement—usually at a higher price.

But buy a good real estate income property and it's profitable for 30, 50, or even 100 years. I've been in hotels in England which were over 400 years old! Sure, the roof had been replaced a few times, candles were snuffed out for electric bulbs, and TV took the place of the court jester. But the walls, floors, doors, and windows are still the same. Just imagine how many lives have been lived out in such a building, how much profit the building earned for its various owners over the years!

Yes, real estate—at least most of it—is financially valuable because it has a long life. Repairs have to be made now and then but the cost of repairs is generally low compared with the value of

---

[2] Available from IWS, Inc., Bank Plaza, Merrick, N.Y. 11566, for $99.50 each.

the property. Yes, you *can* add solid, lasting values to your life by taking over a well-kept piece of income property.

## GET IN ON CONSTANTLY RISING VALUES

We've all heard of hitching our wagon to a star. In real estate you hitch your wagon to a magic money machine. This great money machine constantly—twenty-four hours a day—increases the value of the money you invest in the real estate. Truly in real estate you make money while you sleep!

I know of no other investment that rises in value like real estate. True, the stock market may go up in value for 12, 18, or 24 months. But just as surely as it goes up, so, too, does it go down. You *may* be able to make money in the stock market. If you can, I'm all for you. But plenty of people *don't* make money in the market while millions of people *do* make money in real estate.

Why do so many people make *big* money in real estate? Because they get in on the constantly rising value of well-located and well-built income real estate. You can, too, and I'll show you how.

## WORK THE FEWEST HOURS POSSIBLE

Take over any kind of retail business—such as a travel agency, hardware store, department store, etc., and you'll put in at least 8 hours a day—and more likely 12 hours. But in real estate you can get by on less than half an hour a day—if you organize your income property well.

So why spend 40 to 60 hours a week struggling for an income when you can get the same return in dollars for less than 5 hours' work? Truly, real estate probably requires less time input than any other business known to man! So if you like to work short hours, income real estate is *your* business. What's more, you can make it your spare time business while you hold down a job or run a business in some other field.

## WALK AWAY WITH PROPERTY, CASH, AND INCOME

In real estate you can, with proper planning:

1. Take over property with OPM (Other People's Money)
2. Get extra cash
3. Own the property
4. Never invest a cent of your own

Real estate is one of the few businesses in which you can take over a valuable asset using borrowed money, own the asset, and have extra cash to put in your pocket! The reason for this is that:

- Real estate is an OPM business
- There's always money available for real estate
- Borrowing is "in" in real estate

So if you want to borrow plenty of money without getting a red face over it, then real estate is for you. Keep in mind, at all times, that real estate is the *second* most important item in all our lives, food being first.

### The No-Money-Down Way to Wealth

Another happy reader writes as follows:

> I'm buying my second apartment building with no money down. The first was 42 units for $185,000 with a $25,000 down payment. I got the $25,000 with five $5,000 pyramid loans from five different banks. I've been paying them out of the increased spendable.
>
> My second building is 20 units for $90,000, $9,000 down, a new first loan of $60,000 and the owner will carry the balance of $26,000 plus the loan fee of 1.5 points will be added to the owner's note. On the down payment money on this one, I'm getting the friendly real estate broker to loan me his 6% commission of $5,400 and getting a property improvement loan for $5,000 from a Savings & Loan as you recommended. I'm also carefully timing the close of escrow and prorations of rent to get the owner to make the payments the first month and give me the rent receipts, putting a little extra in my pocket. I plan to raise the rents from $75 to $90 . . . .
>
> "I'm also becoming a business opportunity broker and learning an exciting new career. We charge a minimum $3,000 fee or 10% of the sale price, whichever is greater, on the sale of a business and a 6% fee on the sale of the real estate, or on a net basis. I recently found a drive-in dairy. Listed the business and real estate. The business sold for $16,000 with a $3,000 commission. We had a net listing on the real estate for $75,000 and sold it for $90,000. Business is very good. I very much enjoy the ideas in the IWS Newsletter and other publications. Thanks.

## GO WHERE THE MONEY IS

Real estate is financially important to you, me, our relatives, and friends. To *you*, I want to make real estate as financially important as it has been to *me*. My goal in this book is to make you a real estate millionaire in three years. If you want to stop anywhere short of this goal, that's your decision.

Just remember that everyone needs space—from the hospital bed on which we are born to the six-foot hole in which most of us are finally put to rest. In between we occupy apartments, homes, hotels, motels, and other real estate. And—to date—there is not one human being who can do without real estate.

With the population of our world on its way to doubling, real estate has nowhere to go but up in value. To get in on this worldwide boom, come along with me to learn how *you* can get rich in the world's greatest OPM business.

### Points to Remember

- Prime properties pay profits to *you*.
- Real estate is the best investment made by the average person.
- Real estate is one of the safest businesses known today.
- Your real estate can save you money on your income taxes.
- You can easily grow rich on capital growth in real estate.
- Real estate is a borrowed-money business, meaning that you can get started on zero cash.
- It is easy to get multiple loans on real estate property.
- In real estate you can work just a few hours a week and become a millionaire in three years, or less.

# 2

## HOW TO FINANCE YOUR REAL ESTATE FORTUNE

There are hundreds of ways for *you* to finance *your* real estate fortune. Many of these ways are well-known—they're called *conventional financing.* Other ways are less well-known. You might call these *nonconventional* or *creative financing.* But no matter which way you choose, it can put enormous wealth into *your* pocket. For example, recent deals using these methods:

- Built a $1.2-million real estate fortune in three years on $2,000 of borrowed money
- Put a beginner into a 204-unit apartment development worth $2.85-million without one cent down
- Allowed an experienced real estate operator to take over a 40-story office building with no cash down and walk away with $27,000 in nontaxable cash
- Gave $562,000 cash to a rehabilitation (*rehab* from now on) dealer to improve several properties which were paying him a cash income
- Permitted a 5-year owner of a garden-apartment development to refinance his property to give him nontaxable cash to take over two other profitable properties

- Put a penniless cripple into a rental real estate business in one month, raising his income from zero to $1,200 per month, in 30 days
- Allowed purchase of a $300,000 estate for $546
- Plus many more, which you'll learn about in this chapter, and in later chapters

Now let's first look at conventional financing for new income real estate projects. Hopefully, this book will show up some methods about which you don't know as much as you'd like to. Later we'll look at conventional financing for existing real estate projects.

## MAKE CONVENTIONAL FINANCING WORK FOR YOU

Conventional real estate financing is the money you borrow from sources such as:

- Banks
- Insurance companies
- Mortgage lenders
- Government-backed sources
- Pension funds
- Profit-sharing plans

To make conventional mortgage-money sources work for you, try to:

- Negotiate to get the lowest interest rate
- Avoid paying points (1% of the mortgage per point)
- Use conventional financing for newer income properties whenever possible
- Never let the lender know you're *over-financed*—that is that you've borrowed more than 80% of the funds needed
- Fight against *take-outs* and *sweetners,* or deals in which a lender gets part of the profits (usually 1% or 2% for the life of the project), and perhaps a small piece of the ownership
- Be a complete businessman or woman at all times

Recognize, here and now, that the people you deal with at sources of conventional funds, such as those listed above

- Dislike wheeler-dealers
- Shun mavericks
- Avoid "gunslingers"

This means that, to get conventional financing for your real estate deal, you must:

1. Prepare neat, typed documents
2. Present income and expense statements for each project
3. Fill out all the blanks on the application form
4. Never lose your temper
5. Be ready to make concessions, if they'll make you money
6. Never be afraid of a *No* answer
7. Keep trying one source after another

### CONVENTIONAL MONEY CAN MAKE YOU RICH

A reader who got into rental real estate using my methods writes:

> I have all your books and have just finished reading *Magic Mind Secrets for Building Great Riches Fast.* Also subscribe to IWS and have the "Starting Millionaire" and "Financial Broker" Programs.
>
> I'm now driving a new Cadillac and enjoying the better things in life. _____ Bank told me to bring them some more professional people with good statements and they would lend me down-payments all day long. (This reader wrote this after getting multiple loans to finance his first zero-cash property). I'm getting ready to buy my second $200,000 building across the street. Many thanks for a better way of life and an opportunity to put into practice principles that really work.

### YOU CAN GET MILLIONS

Conventional mortgage money sources can furnish you millions of dollars for your real estate projects. Some such sources lend a minimum of $1-million for their loans; others set their minimum at $2-million, or $5-million. So we're not talking about peanuts.

To latch onto these millions you, in general, must:

• Have a new or relatively new income project in real estate
• Have a good income potential from this real estate
• Carry adequate insurance on the property

You can also say that, *in general*, conventional loan sources:

• Dislike projects in slum or run-down areas

- May avoid way-out projects—like mobile homes, trailer parks, marinas, etc.
- Can make you sweat for your money longer than other sources of funds

But don't turn off conventional funds. Why? The answer is a five-letter word—*money*! Keep in mind at all times this Hickism:

> Be friendly, sweet, and engaging to every source of big money. You never know when you'll need big money and having a friend at the bank costs you nothing!

### MAKE CONVENTIONAL MONEY MAKE YOU RICH

Most of the conventional money sources listed above usually prefer long-term mortgage loans—15 years, or more. But you'll find that, at certain times, insurance companies will lend *short-term money* for:

- Building construction
- Interim financing
- Stand-by purposes

Knowing how each of these financing arrangements works can help make you rich.

*Building construction* loans cover only the putting up of a structure. As such, these loans run for about three years, or less. The money may be paid directly to you or to the contractor doing the work, after you've certified that the work is finished satisfactorily. On large jobs, you will usually have your lender make payments after completion of certain percentages of the work—20%, 40%, 60%, etc. Some banks dislike construction loans because too much can go wrong during construction to cause problems and the possible loss of the borrowed money. Construction funds are usually high cost—typically 10%, or more.

To use these facts to make big money from conventional funds:

- Don't, unless a bank specifically advertises the availability of construction funds, ask a bank for a loan for this purpose.
- Remember that once you get off on the wrong foot with a bank, it takes a long time to set things right again.
- Keep an eye open for construction funds at all times.

*Interim financing* covers the time from the start of construction of a real estate project until you get long-term financing. Thus, your interim financing can cover:

- Buying the land
- Breaking ground
- Construction
- First few months' operation

To show you how this method works for you, here's a beautifully profitable way to get started in real estate in multi–dwelling condominiums (condos for short) on 100% interim financing–that is without investing a cent of your own. Here are the steps you can take:

1. Find a suitable piece of land for your proposed condo
2. Get interim financing for the price of the land plus 10 to 25% or more to cover unforseen costs
3. Have plans prepared for the building you are planning to put up on the land. (You may need sketch plans to get the financing mentioned in Step 2–the usual cost of such plans is $500, or less).
4. Advertise the units for sale. (Typical prices range from $10,000 to as high as $100,000, or more, per unit, depending on the building, its location, the floor the unit is on, etc.)
5. Collect the down payments in cash from the buyers of the units
6. Obtain from the lender or mortgagor (this is the organization that lends to you and is usually a bank) the credit for the balance of the sale price of each unit

### KNOW HOW IT WORKS IN REAL LIFE[1]

Now let's look at a real-life example of this technique as it was used recently in a southern state condominium put up with 100% plus financing. This 12-story building is to be built on a waterfront property that has a price of $120,000. You visit a local architect and have him prepare a sketch plan of a building containing 80

---

[1]To work a deal such as this you *must* have an attorney and you *must* follow all Federal (SEC) and State Laws.

units (each of which is a complete apartment) having an average price of $35,000. The construction cost is estimated to be $2.4-million. A one-third, or $11,550 average down payment will be made by each purchaser of one unit or apartment in this condominium. The local bank agrees to finance the remainder of each unit.

You are required by the seller of the land to pay 60%, or $72,000 cash, with the remainder being financed by a five-year *purchase-money* (called P.M.) mortgage given you by the seller. This means that he is willing to finance $48,000 of the $120,000 price of the land. So your task is to come up with $72,000 cash, to put down on the land. Once you do this you can start selling units. So here's how you handle the deal:

1. You borrow $72,000 interim money from a bank or an insurance company to put down on the land. (This interim money is sometimes called a *development loan* when used for this purpose).
2. At the same time, another bank or insurance company gives you a written promise to lend you 80% of the construction money you need, or 0.80 ($2.4-million) = $1.92-million. (The same bank or insurance firm that lends you the interim money might also make the construction loan).
3. As soon as you have the land you start advertising the units.
4. Within one week you sell 30 units, which gives you 30 ($11,550) = $346,500 in cash, plus the mortgages on these 30 units. (Note that the mortgages are *promises* by the bank or other lender to pay you, the owner, for the unit when the building is finished.
5. You hold the $346,500 cash for use as operating capital while the building is being put up. Note that within a short time after taking over the land, you have cash in hand.
6. You now have $1,920,000 + 346,500 = $2,266,500 available to you from the construction loan and the cash down payments on the units you sold. Also, you'll receive $703,500 in cash from the units you sold, when they are occupied. Thus, your cash inflow will be $2,970,000. This

compares with a total cost of $2,400,000 + 120,000 = $2,520,000. And remember that you still have 50 units available for sale!

This real-life deal shows you a number of facts about conventional money sources for real estate, namely, that such sources:

- Are loaded with potential wealth for you
- Can be tapped easily if you plan carefully
- Are excellent reservoirs of 100% financing of your real estate deal
- Have *billions* available for *your* deal—if you work hard!

### Hard Work Pays Off in Real Estate

Yes, hard work *does* pay off in real estate. For, as one reader writes:

> Approximately one year ago I purchased your book *How to Borrow Your Way to a Great Fortune.*
>
> The results speak for themselves.
> $3,000,000 of properties "sales arranged" in _____ .
> Thus far in _____, confirmed sales of $3,500,000 of mobile home parks . . . nursing homes, income property . . . plus $5,000,000 of hospitals and a million dollars of nursing homes on tap.
> After reading your book, my initial letterhead cost $6.50, and the present letterhead and other mailing pieces as developed are attached. Thus, anyone can do it.
> Other than your book we have had some great lifts from friends . . . real friends, that is . . . But the results speak . . . and, of course, lots of hard work . . . 4-8 letters a week . . . developing forms, etc . . . . It was all worth it and plenty of prayers to a wife and family of sons willing to put up with it all . . . All of us a lot better for it . . . . Keep up the good work.

### EXPAND YOUR 100% FINANCING BY ONE-THIRD

The first deal above shows you an important aspect of modern real estate which most people never learn, namely:

The average value of a completed commercial real estate property today is often one-third more than its total cost, including the land. This general rule applies to apartment houses, shopping centers, motels, hotels, office buildings and similar structures.

Let's take a look at how this can work out for you if you put up structures having various total costs, including the land. You will, I'm sure, be impressed with the magic "grow power" of other people's money (OPM) available to you from conventional mortgage money sources.

| Cost of Completed Project | Value of Completed Project |
|---|---|
| $   900,000 | $  1,200,000 |
| 1,200,000 | 1,600,000 |
| 1,800,000 | 2,400,000 |
| 2,400,000 | 3,200,000 |
| 3,000,000 | 4,000,000 |
| 3,600,000 | 4,800,000 |
| 4,200,000 | 5,600,000 |
| 6,000,000 | 8,000,000 |
| 9,000,000 | 12,000,000 |
| 12,000,000 | 16,000,000 |
| 15,000,000 | 20,000,000 |
| 21,000,000 | 28,000,000 |

So, to find the probable sale value of any completed real estate project, just take one-third of the total cost of the completed project, including the land, and add this to the cost of the project. While this rule may vary a trifle from one area to another, you can be reasonably sure that the value of your project will rise:

- During the time of construction
- Because of your development efforts
- As a result of increased labor, material, and land costs

Thus, time and nature are on *your* side when you use OPM and 100% financing from conventional real estate money sources to put up a project. Further, you *can* wind up with 110% to 130% financing, meaning that:

- You walk away with tax-free cash in your pocket
- You can (or may, if you wish) retain ownership of all, or some, of the property

- You have the beginnings of a new real estate empire using OPM, the difference being that the second time around you need not be so hungry!

So, for the moment at least, let's glance away from conventional financing of real estate deals and look at nonconventional financing arrangements. But before we go, let's remember that conventional financing is usually, or:

- Persnickety—requiring many forms, long discussions, precise contracts, etc.
- Is the way to go when you have first-class projects
- Can provide you with, and make you, a bundle of money
- Seldom gets you into money troubles that may come with being overfinanced

Yes, conventional OPM is the dream way to riches in real estate. But don't buy it 100 percent until after you've looked at nonconventional sources of real estate funds.

### Go All the Way in Your Wealth Building

Conventional real estate money sources can lead to all sorts of wealth. For instance, the reader who wrote to me to say: "Your work has been an inspiration to me lately. Although I had the so-called "academic fame" previously now I am a donator (to academic causes), company president as well as everything else and feel pretty good about it. In less than a year after reading your book, I now have my own company, own 200 acres of land, two apartment houses which bring in rent, a co-op in Sutton Place[2], and a computer! I am also going into the trading business in cosmetics and wigs."

### GET YOUR MONEY FASTER BUT PAY MORE

Nonconventional sources of real estate funds include:

- Money brokers
- Private lenders
- Investment trusts
- Limited partnerships
- Finders

---

[2]One of the most expensive and most exclusive residential areas in the world.

- Corporate lenders
- Finance companies

There are other nonconventional sources which we'll mention as we go along. For a full coverage of the newest and most active nonconventional sources of real estate funds, be sure to read regularly the monthly newsletter for all wealth builders—beginning and experienced—*International Wealth Success*. To get this excellent newsletter, which often presents:

- 100% 110%, 115%, and more, financing (money) sources
- Compensating-balance loan sources
- New wealth ideas every month
- Many, many sources of business loans
- Part-time money-making ideas
- Mail-order riches opportunities
- Hundreds of finders fee listings
- Worldwide international money-making ideas
- Fast-fortune easy-money wealth deals
- Franchise riches ideas and methods
- Capital available for borrowers of all types
- Monthly Ty Hicks page where Ty talks to *you*
- Financial broker opportunities
- Thousands of other ideas, sources and ways to earn big money and make your fortune today!
- Ways to get money you need
- Unique techniques to earn big money
- Secrets that put cash in your pocket

send $24 to IWS Inc., Bank Plaza, Merrick, NY 11566. Now let's look at how the usual nonconventional sources can put big bucks of OPM into your realty pocket. But first we'll take a quick look at how some folks get their loans.

**Get the Loans You Need**

Sometimes readers tell a simple, short story in two or three sentences, such as this one written to the editors of IWS. "Keep up the good work. I have already received one loan through your paper. I am on my way!"

### USE MONEY BROKERS TO THE HILT

Money brokers bring you and money sources together, just like a marriage broker brings the boy and girl together to make—hopefully—a happy union. My observations of a number of money and marriage brokers is that people are usually happier with the results they obtain from their money brokers than from their marriage brokers!

Now you probably have a number of questions for me concerning money brokers and I'm ready to answer them here and now I hope that *your* questions are amongst those answered below.

#### Money-Broker Questions and Answers

*Q.*    Why should I use a money broker?

*A.*    There are several reasons why you should at least *consider* using a money broker, including:

- Easier loans
- Faster loans
- Less investigation
- Money for marginal properties
- Multiple loans possible
- Numerous sources
- Few geographical limitations

*Q.*    Do money brokers charge higher rates?

*A.*    Yes, you will *usually* have to pay higher interest rates for the real estate funds you borrow from money brokers. But the interest *rate* is unimportant if:

- You can make a profit on the money
- You can attain your goals
- You're better off with the money than without the money

Keep one fact in mind about interest rates:

> As long as you can make a profit on borrowed money the rate of interest you pay is unimportant because the interest is both provable and tax-deductible.

A further very important concept is this: *You pay your bills with dollars, not with percent signs.* So what you seek in real estate—if you use my methods—is spendable dollars, not low interest rates!

*Q.* Why are money brokers important to me?

*A.* Because, with conventional financing you put up at least one dollar for every three dollars the mortgage lender puts up—in the usual deal. But with a money broker you will usually put up zero dollars for every dollar the broker puts up. True, you have to pay more for the broker's money. But when a BWB is just starting, he or she is "hungry"—and a hungry person will do almost anything honest for some good food. So, too, the BWB, but the name of his food is bucks.

*Q.* Where can I get the names and addresses of reliable money lenders and brokers with cash in hand for me?

*A.* The two best sources I know of are *International Wealth Success,* mentioned earlier, and the big money book, *Business Capital Sources,* available at $15 from IWS at the above address. This book lists thousands of money sources from which you might borrow 100%, or more, of the money you need for profitable real estate deals.

*Q.* Why is it easier for me to borrow from a money broker?

*A.* It is easier for you to borrow from a money broker because he or she:

- Will take greater risks
- Wheels and deals faster
- Requires little, or no, collateral
- Understands you better

Of course, your money broker will charge you more for your loan. But if you can bank your profits, or put them into other, bigger deals, who cares about the higher charge? Remember this:

When you borrow money to make money, the interest you pay is nothing more than "rent" for the use of money to make money!

So if you're paying 10% interest to a money broker (and this is a typical charge), you're paying 10¢ a year to rent one dollar. But if you can earn 20¢ or 25¢ a year on each borrowed dollar you put into real estate, then a money broker's charge is low, compared to your potential profit on the deal.

As a general guide you can say that there are few times when conventional financing beats the money broker. One is:

> Most banks are usually legally allowed to give 100% financing on real estate when they have foreclosed (taken over because of lack of payments) on a property. The 100% financed property may be your best possible deal because you don't put a penny down.

There are, of course, 110%, 120%, 130%, etc., financing deals in which you get more cash than you need at the moment. But you can't put these together just with conventional funds. You need the help of a money broker's or some other lender's bucks. How do I know? Because I specialize in putting together the money end of such deals for people. The biggest *mortgaging out* or *windfall* deal I ever heard of was 162%—the buyer walked away with $620,000 in cash after taking over a $1-million building without a penny down! We'll talk more about that later. The buyer used a money broker to the hilt, just as we advised earlier.

### SEARCH OUT PRIVATE LENDERS

If you could sit with me and listen to the money complaints I hear, you'd cry tears of joy. Why? Because the people I deal with are sometimes wildly looking for:

- Good investments for their millions of dollars of surplus cash
- Borrowers who will put other people's money (OPM) to work in a safe, creative, and profitable way

As president of an over $3-million asset money lending organization, I have to listen to the monthly bellyaches of my board of directors saying:

- *When* will we make more loans?
- *How* can we make more loans?
- *Who* can we find to borrow our money?
- *How* can we get people to borrow more money from us?

- *Why* are we losing loans to the competition?
- *What* kinds of offers can we make to people to get them to give us their loan business?

Truly, this organization, of which I am currently president, is loaded with money which we can lend to our members for all good deals, such as:

- Real estate
- Personal purchases
- Auto, boat, equipment financing
- Debt consolidation
- Other

Yet we worry and worry as to why we can't make more good loans! Each month we try to make more loans than the previous month. And each year we try to beat the previous year by making more loans to more people for more purposes for which more of our loan money is needed!

True, we grow each year—but not as fast as we'd like to. And why is this? Because our rate of growth is held down by the intense loan competition from:

- Private lenders
- Banks
- Finance companies
- Credit unions
- Other

But of all the competition, the private lenders may—we think—give us the worst battle.

## IDENTIFY THE PRIVATE LENDERS

And who are these private lenders? They are the wealthy and the not-so-wealthy people of this world who want to put their excess cash to work earning better than bank rates. For instance, the usual private lender receives 10%-18% a year on his loans to corporations. Some smart private lenders even get a piece of the real estate action from an *equity kicker* during tight money times. (An equity kicker is a small share in the profits of a property, plus a small percentage of the ownership and—possibly—a share in the capital-gains profit on the sale of the property.) Now for some questions.

*Q.* Where can I locate private lenders?

*A.* Here are a few publications that carry ads or notices of private lenders looking for a safe "home" for their funds:

- *International Wealth Success*
- *Wall Street Journal*
- *New York Times*
- The book *Business Capital Sources*
- The book *Worldwide Riches Opportunities*, Vol. 2 (lists foreign lenders)

*Q.* How do I approach a private lender?

*A.* There are various ways to approach a private lender. One of the best I know of—and one that has worked beautifully for thousands of BWBs—is this:

> When a prospective lender asks you: "Where did you get our name?" reply: "You were recommended to me by an outstanding financial adviser," if you have consulted such an adviser.

Such a reply is a compliment to the lender and puts him on *your* side. Using such a reply:

- Gives you a greater chance of getting the loan
- Makes your dealings more cordial
- Reduces the possibility of arguments and hard feelings

Never, never tell a lender: "Oh, I found your name in a list of lenders." This is the surest way to turn off a lender. And it can lead to a *No* answer in situations where you would get a *Yes* if you used the response given above.

*Q.* Can private lenders *really* help me?

*A.* Positively, yes! The private lender can put you in the chips faster than you think. So don't overlook the private lender. He can be the difference between riches and poverty, for you!

## WILL AN INVESTMENT TRUST HELP YOU?

Real estate is fortunate in many ways, including:

- Plenty of other people's money
- High leverage on this money
- Fantastic appreciation in value
- Regular income to owner
- A basic need of everyone
- Is almost foolproof
- Can be set up as a trust

A *real estate investment trust,* (called REIT for short) can put bundles of money into your real estate pocket. What's more, a REIT pays *NO* Federal income taxes if it distributed 90%, or more, of its income, after expenses. And, of course, one of the expenses of a REIT could be *your* annual salary.

### Reit Questions and Answers

*Q.* What is a REIT?

*A.* A REIT is a trust set up to invest in real estate—either by operating, lending for, or otherwise earning a profit from real estate. A REIT is not allowed to own real estate directly. However, it can earn large profits from its investments in real estate.

*Q.* How and where does a REIT get money?

*A.* A REIT sells shares of *beneficial* interest, much like stock shares, to the public. Thus, a REIT recently sold 1.2 million shares at $25 each giving a total cash inflow of nearly $30-million to the REIT. (The underwriting fees are paid out of the proceeds of the offering.) This REIT is a mortgage trust—that is, its funds will be invested in real estate mortgages at a profitable rate of interest.

*Q.* Must a REIT go for millions of dollars?

*A.* No; you can have a trust that takes in only a small amount of money—say $300,000 or $500,000. The amount of money sought depends upon the goals of the REIT.

*Q.* Can I form a REIT?

*A.* You certainly can! All you need is the knowhow.

*Q.* Where can I get this knowhow?

*A.* Later in this book you will find more information on the formation of a REIT. You can obtain additional information from the IWS *"Starting Millionaire" Program* available from IWS at $99.50 at the address given earlier in this chapter. Just keep in mind the fact that a REIT can put millions of dollars of OPM into your bank for use in real estate ventures.

### Luck Comes to Those Ready for It

Many BWBs think they are "unlucky." Yet my experience in life shows that luck comes to those who are ready for it. Like this reader who says:

> I started this shop with one ad in the paper for a 6% loan and a 5% finders fee—got two $100,000 offers within one week. Was scratching my head on which to take, and what to do with the excess capital, when a relative left me enough to do the job comfortably. God helps those that help themselves, I guess—but things like this never happened to me before knowing you and venturing out with some of your ideas and suggestions.

### MAKE A LIMITED PARTNERSHIP PAY OFF

The *limited partnership* (LP) is a popular way to finance real estate—from one building to an entire complex of structures. In a LP, two or more *general partners* operate the business. *Limited partners* contribute money to the LP (generally in amounts of $5,000, or more, each) but do not take part in the business operation at all. Further, if there is a business failure or disaster of some sort, the liability of each limited partner is restricted to his or her contribution to the LP. Other advantages of the LP are:

- Fast raising of real estate funds
- Control of project is retained
- Easy legal requirements
- Few operating problems

To form a LP, all you need do is prepare the LP agreement, register it with your county clerk or other responsible official, and take the necessary steps to sell participations in the LP. While this seems simple, remember this fact at all times:

> You must, must have an attorney help you form and market a LP. If you do not use an attorney, you can get into serious business problems.

Now how much money might you raise with a LP? The amount of money you can raise can range from as little as $10,000 to as much as $50-million, or more. What you can raise depends on the:

- Number of participations offered
- Price per participation
- Number of participations sold
- Selling expenses involved

For a typical LP agreement and the type of ads used to promote such firms, see the IWS *"Starting Millionaire" Program* mentioned above. You can also check with your attorney to have him show you what is required in a LP agreement. The *"Starting Millionaire" Program* mentioned above contains a full-length example of a LP agreement for a typical real estate venture. You will also find LP data in two other IWS courses, namely: *"Fast Financing of Real Estate Fortunes,"* and the *"Real Estate Fortune Builders Course."* Each is priced at $99.50.

## USE FINDERS TO GET YOUR MONEY

A *finder* is a person or firm who, or which, *finds* things that other people or firms seek, and for which they are willing to pay a finders fee. Thus, you can ask a finder to locate money which you can borrow and invest in real estate. You don't have to pay the finders fee until *after* you obtain the money you seek.

Now where can you locate a finder? That's easy. Just run a free ad in the monthly newsletter *International Wealth Success.* Any one-year subscriber is entitled to run as many free ads as he or she wishes to, and for which space is available.

The usual finders fee will run between 1% and 5% of the money obtained for you. You pay a lower percentage as the amount of money obtained increases.

## CORPORATE LENDERS ARE LOADED

Millions of corporations around the world are loaded with excess cash they'd like to invest. Certain of these corporations are willing to invest their money in real estate.

To locate corporate lenders, search the *Capital Available* and *Mortgages* columns of:

- *International Wealth Success*
- *The Wall Street Journal*
- *The New York Times*
- Large newspapers in your area
- The book *Business Capital Sources*

You must be constantly alert to find suitable corporate lenders. But these sources have so much money that the time you put in is well worth the effort. We'll talk some more about corporate lenders in later chapters.

## FINANCE COMPANIES CAN HELP YOU, TOO

The finance company most of us know is the small firm that lends $800, $1500, or some other pittance to people who need money to tide them over a few rough spots. Yet there are giant finance companies which lend millions for real estate. You can find many of these finance companies listed in the sources given above for corporate lenders.

You will usually pay higher interest rates to finance companies and corporate lenders. But if you're just getting started in real estate, you can't be too choosy about who opens his or her purse to you. Later, when you have your real estate empire, you can pick and choose among lenders who want your mortgage business. You may even complain to me that "people are trying to throw at me money I don't want! How can I make them stop?" The day *you* come to me with such complaints I'll be very happy for you!

## YES, YOU CAN BORROW YOUR WAY TO WEALTH

Real estate has many "beauties" for the BWB. Probably the most important one is that borrowed money is "the way of life" in real estate. So if you're short of cash—and plenty of people seem to be—consider using real estate as *your* way to great wealth.

This chapter has shown you a few sources of ready cash for financing *your* real estate fortune. Now let's get busy earning that fortune for you!

### Points to Remember

- You *can* borrow your way to a real estate fortune quickly and easily.
- Conventional money sources (banks, insurance companies, etc.) can make you rich in real estate.
- The day you finish putting up a new real estate project it may be worth 30 percent more than you paid for it with OPM.
- You may get real estate money faster from nonconventional sources but it may cost you more in interest.
- Money brokers, private lenders, finders, and corporations are a few other sources of real estate loans.
- Real estate is a borrowed-money business—which makes it easier for you to get the loans you need.

# 3

## YOUR KEYS TO FIVE THOUSAND SOURCES OF READY REAL ESTATE MONEY

Real estate offers you many, many chances to get richer faster. And one of the main reasons for this is:

Real estate is a *borrowed-money business!* Hardly any real estate deals are ever closed for cash.

This means that it is almost always easy for *you* to get the borrowed money you need to put a real estate deal together. But you *must* know *where* and *how* to get borrowed money! Knowledge is power!

### GO THE WAY OF 100% FINANCING

Lots of real estate deals are closed with 100% financing. When this happens, the buyer—such as yourself:

- Puts up *NO* MONEY at all
- Takes over valuable property for *NO* CASH

- May *GET CASH* for taking over a valuable property
- Often gets a monthly income from the property
- Seldom has to pay cash for legal expenses (you should *always* have an attorney when buying real estate)

"Ty," you say, "this sounds too good to be true! How, and where, can *I* get the money to work such deals?"
I'll answer your questions this way:

1. Such deals may sound "too good to be true," but they can happen every business day of the year in this great land of ours!
2. You can—I'm almost positive—get the money for these deals from one or more of the sources I'll give you in this chapter!

So forget all the negative talk about your not being able to get the money you need that you may have heard from people who'd rather "yack" than "do." For I'm telling *you*—here and now—that:

> You *can* get the real estate money you need—if you use the hints I give you here.

### REAL ESTATE MONEY IS EVERYWHERE

And how can I be so sure *you* can get the money *you* need? That's easy. Thousands of my readers have written or told me—or both—that they got the real estate money they needed, using my methods. A few standout readers I remember include:

- A BWB who was $12,500 in debt and full of failure. Yet while reading one of my books he found the key to his future real estate wealth. Using my methods, he was able to build a garden-type apartment complex firm, starting with no cash of his own. In just 24 short months he went from $12,500 in debt to the ownership of a real estate firm worth nearly $2-million—starting with *no cash* of his own. His letter describing this wonderful experience, and thanking me for the help my books gave him, is in my reader letter file for anyone who wants to read it. "I owe you an eternal debt of gratitude for what you've done for me," the letter says, in part.

• Two BWBs from New England took over some 100 rental units for no cash down, no legal fee payout, no closing costs, no other out-of-pocket expenses. These two young BWBs walked away from the closing (called the "passing" in their state) with $1,400 in their pockets and the income from the rental units starting to come in the *next* day. Also, they took over rent security deposits of several thousand dollars. While you are not allowed to spend such deposits, putting them into your business bank account will sure help you to win friends at *your* bank! Try it and see for yourself!

I could continue with case after case. But these two should convince you that:

> You can get started in real estate today on borrowed money without putting up a penny of your own!

During a recent year of "tight money" (a period when it is more difficult than usual to find lenders), more than $30-billion was loaned for real estate, just in the United States. If you were to include loans in the rest of the world, more than $500-billion was loaned on real estate in just one tight-money year! That's a bundle of money. (Remember, friend, that a billion is a thousand million!) And *you* can easily make some of that *yours*—even in tight money times!

## HOW TO FIND THE RIGHT REAL ESTATE LENDER

There are many types of real estate lenders. These include:

• Commercial banks
• Savings and loan associations
• Mutual savings banks
• Mortgage companies
• Insurance firms
• Federal and State lenders
• Real estate investment trusts
• Mortgage bankers
• Private lenders
• Pension funds
• Large corporations

These lenders may make all or some of the following types of real estate loans:

- First, second, third, etc., mortgage loans
- Construction loans
- Land loans
- Standby loans
- Takeout loans
- Property improvement loans
- Bridging loans
- Utility (sewer, sidewalk, electric) loans
- Takeover loans
- Refinancing loans
- Development loans
- Property expansion loans
- Permanent financing loans

You now know what types of lenders make real estate loans and the kinds of loans you can get for real estate use. The lenders you seek can be found:

- In this book
- In other books I'll recommend to you
- In real estate magazines

To help you out immediately, I'm listing in this chapter some 60 active real estate lenders. To give you a variety of sources, I've picked banks, insurance companies, real estate investment trusts, mortgage firms, etc., which were actively making real estate loans at the time this book was written.

And—as a further service to you—I've picked these lenders from a variety of geographic areas. Why did I do this? Because no matter what a lender tells you:

Many real estate lenders prefer to make local loans—at least for the first loan they make to a borrower.

So try a lender in your state, or a nearby state first. You just may get the money *you* need on your first try—as some of my readers have. Now here's your list of active real estate lenders. Another advantage you will gain from the following list is a "taste" of the variety of firms making real estate loans.

Where a statement appears after the name and address of a lender, the wording is that of the lender, as of the time of this writing—not my wording. I think you'll find the list both interesting *and* useful.

## REAL ESTATE CAPITAL SOURCES

Union Dime Savings Bank, Avenue of the Americas at 40th St., New York, NY 10018. 212-221-2000.

Howard S. Bissell, Investment Plaza, Cleveland, OH 44114. 216-621-3383. Nationwide real estate financing.

Gould Investors Trust, 245 Great Neck Rd., Great Neck, NY 11021. 561-446-3100. Real estate investments throughout the United States.

Feist & Feist, 58 Park Place, Newark, NJ 07102. 201-643-8500. In Orlando, FL, 504 Pan American Bank Bldg., Orlando, FL 32801. 305-425-3484. One of America's largest and most active "full-service" real estate companies.

Gulf Coast Investment Corporation, 1903 Hermann Drive, Houston, TX 77004.

First Federal Savings, 3003 North Central Ave., Phoenix, AZ 85012. 602-248-4120.

Sutro Mortgage Investment Trust, 4900 Wilshire Blvd., Los Angeles, CA 90010. 213-937-4000.

L.J. Restieri, 445 Northern Blvd., Great Neck, NY 11021. 516-829-5150. 1st and 2nd mortgages, SBIC loans, shopping centers, office buildings, apartment houses within 200 miles of New York City.

Firstmark Credit Corp., 110 E. Washington, Indianapolis, IN 46204. 317-632-5379. Commercial second mortgages; competitive rates; 5-year loans with or without amortization.

Brooks, Harvey & Co., Inc., 280 Park Ave., New York, NY 10017. 212-687-1920. Creative financing and consulting for major real estate projects.

Pence Mortgage Company, 2840 One Indiana Square, Indianapolis, IN 46204. 317-635-1307. Commercial, industrial, residential real estate financing.

BA Mortgage Company of Minnesota, Northwestern Financial Center, Minneapolis, MN 55431. 612-835-1150. Offer the developer/borrower an entire range of real estate financing services.

Charter Investment & Development Company, 600 Bank for Savings Building, Birmingham, AL 35202. 205-328-9441. One of the largest financial organizations in the nation.

Mellon National Mortgage Co. of Ohio, 1255 Euclid Ave., Suite 500, Cleveland, OH 44115. 216-696-5432. Specialists in creative mortgage financing.

Bob Bassel Realties, 640 Cathcart St., Montreal, Quebec, Canada, H3B 1M3. Cash available for immediate commitment.

Collins Tuttle and Company, 261 Madison Ave., New York, NY 10016. 212-MU-2-4020.

Heitman Mortgage Company, 4408 IDS Center, Minneapolis, MN 55402. 612-336-1603.

Conservative Mortgage Company, 1200 Roanoke Bldg., Minneapolis, MN 55402. 612-339-8821. Intermediate term loans, standby commitments, permanent takeouts, construction loans, etc.

Indiana Mortgage Company, Market Square Center, 151 N. Delaware St., Indianapolis, IN 46266. "We'll help you get started."

Cooper-Horowitz Inc., 342 Madison Ave., New York, NY 10017. 212-986-8400. Real estate financing.

Underwood Mortgage and Title Co., 1150 Springfield Ave., Irvington, NJ 07111. You'll find us fast and sure with our commitments.

Univest, Inc., 500 W. Wilson Bridge Rd., Worthington, OH 43085. 614-888-5353. Real estate investments created and funded.

Mortgage & Financial Resources, Inc., 1008 Tower Building, Seattle, WA 98101. 206-624-3326.

Bell & Crane Mortgage Loans, Inc., 1210 Kanawha Valley Building, Charleston, W VA 25301.

Coronado Mortgage Corporation Ltd., 210 Bank of Montreal Bldg., 2609 Granville St., Vancouver, B.C. Canada. 604-736-6545. Complete financial service.

Continental Resources Incorporated, 720 Fox Pavilion, Jenkintown, PA 19046. 215-886-0290. Unlimited funds available—nationwide.

Trust Mortgage Corporation, Banco de Ponce Bldg., Suite 800, Hato Rey, Puerto Rico 00918. 809-767-0059. Knowledge, experience and service.

R & G Mortgage Corp., GPO Box 2394, San Juan, PR 00936. 809-722-4895.

Weaver Bros., Inc., 5530 Wisconsin Ave., Washington, D.C. 20015. 301-986-4000. Interim and permanent financing.

Glasser Mortgage Company, 16 East 52nd St., New York, NY 10022. 212-247-4210. Analyze, process, and make a proposal within 48 hours.

Citizens Mortgage Corporation, 24700 Northwestern Highway, Southfield, MI 48075. 313-354-1100. Ready to finance any sound real estate project, anywhere in the U.S.

Conservative Mortgage Company, 1200 Roanoke Building, Minneapolis, MN 55402. 612-339-8821. Specialists in real estate financing.

Dominion Mortgage Corporation, 1000 Ponce de Leon Blvd., Coral Gables, FL 33134. 305-446-3111. The more than money money company.

Conco Mortgage Company, 50 California St., San Francisco, CA 94111. 415-788-1818. Provides the means for getting the latest input on financing requirements.

Keystone Mortgage Company, 11340 W. Olympic Blvd., Los Angeles, CA 90064. 213-479-4121. Before planting your seed money, plan your long-term financing here.

The Charterhouse Financial Group, 2337 Lemoine Ave., Fort Lee, NJ 07024. 201-947-9414. Any type mortgage or joint venture; no geographic limitations.

United California Mortgage Co., 245 S. Los Robles, Panorama City, CA 91109. 213-578-7600.

American National Bank & Trust Co., 33 N. LaSalle St., Chicago, ILL 60690.

Maine Guarantee Authority, State House, Augusta ME 04430.

G.M.A.I., Inc., 11 Grace Ave. Great Neck, NY 11021. 516-829-8630. Permanent loans; second mortgage loans; construction loans; land acquisition.

Pearce, Mayer & Green, Inc., 90 Park Ave., New York, NY 10016. 212-682-1400. Specialists in long-term, short-term and construction financing.

The Kissell Company, 30 Warder St., Springfield, OH 45501. 513-325-7651. There are so many good mortgage bankers, we have to be better.

UNF Corporation, 745 Fifth Ave., New York, NY 10022. 212-758-9200. Second mortgage loans nationally—apartment houses, office buildings, shopping centers, industrials.

The Galbreath Mortgage Company, 101 E. Town St., Columbus, OH 43215. 614-228-3000. Permanent and construction financing for residential, commercial and large scale FHA projects.

James Talcott, Inc., Mortgage Loan Division, 1290 Avenue of the Americas, New York, NY 10019. 212-956-2873.

Eberhardt Company, 3250 W. 66th St., Minneapolis, MN 55440. 612-920-9280. Financing finesse; complete professional real estate and financing services.

Hammond Economic Development Commission, 5925 Calumet Ave., Hammond, IN 46320. 219-853-6301. Up to $5-million tax exempt bond financing available to qualified business, industry, and developers.

Jersey Mortgage Company, 430 Westfield Ave., Elizabeth, NJ 07201. 201-354-8000. "We have the money . . . the experience . . . the imagination."

National City Bank, 623 Euclid Ave., Cleveland, OH 44114. 216-861-4900. We'll make your loan any way you want it. And anywhere in the U.S.A.

Standard Financial Corporation, 277 Park Ave., New York, NY 10017. 212-922-4660. First mortgage standby commitments and construction financing. Bankable standby commitments to cover first mortgage gap conditions. Second mortgages on income producing properties.

Republic National Life Insurance Co., 3988 N. Central Expressway, Dallas, TX 75204.

Realty and Mortgage Investors of the Pacific (RAMPAC), 44 Montgomery St., San Francisco, CA 94140. 415-398-5721. Short, intermediate, standing, junior, and long-term mortgages.

Sidney N. Weniger Organizations, 745 Fifth Ave., New York, NY 10022. 212-PL-2-8300. "Engineered financing."

Home State Savings Association, 601 Main St., Cincinnati, OH 45202. 513-721-3400. Stand-by commitments for all types of real estate developments.

Stanton L. Triester International Investment & Financial Corp., 1700 Market St., Philadelphia, PA 19103. 215-LO-4-1000. Real estate loans and financing available.

Amortibanc Investment Company, Inc., Garvey Center, 300 West Douglas, Wichita, KS 67202. 316-263-1161. Financing arranged for everything in real estate.

Investors Funding Corporation of New York, 630 Fifth Avenue, New York, NY 10036. 212-333-4000. Funds available for real estate and mortgages anywhere in the U.S.A.

Dovenmuehle, Inc., 135 S. LaSalle St., Chicago, ILL 60604. 312-AN-3-2200. Mortgage financing.

NFC Mortgage Corporation, 301 Almeria Ave., Miami, FL 33134. 305-444-8411. A dynamic leader in its field, NFC offers 100% financing for new condo construction or rental conversions.

American Fletcher Mortgage Company, 600 American Fletcher Building, Indianapolis, IN 46204. 317-633-2443. Total "package financing."

## MORE REAL ESTATE LENDERS FOR YOU

I'm a great believer in a number of business methods which have made me more than a million dollars. These methods are:

- Work *fast*—grow *fast*—build *fast*
- Do your own research—quickly
- Buy—and use—good business books
- Learn fast—act fast
- Never give up—you are *never* too old!
- Use your head at *all* times
- Expand your knowhow and fill your pockets

Most of these methods are covered elsewhere in this book. So in this chapter I'd like to list for you a number of good business books which—in some cases—contain the names and addresses of real estate lenders. These books are so useful that I call them your *Keys* to 5,000 sources of ready real estate money. I'm certain they'll get you the real estate money you seek. These books—which can be your keys to real estate wealth—are:

From The Institute for Business Planning, IBP Plaza, Englewood Cliffs, NJ 07632: Casey, W.J.—*Successful Financing Techniques That Boost Real Estate Sales And Profits.* $39.50. 375 pg, 8.5 x 11 in. Gives useful info on the financing of real estate. Does not list the names and addresses of specific lenders.

Casey, W.J.—*Real Estate Investment Planning.* $60.000, 700 pg. 8.5 x 11 in. Covers a variety of topics, including financing, leasing, depreciation, syndicates, trusts, public corporations, etc. Does not list the names and addresses of lenders.

Casey, W.J.—*Real Estate Desk Book.* $27.50, 400 pg, 5 3/8 x 8 in. Covers financing, land development, figuring values, tax knowhow, etc., without giving the names and addresses of lenders.

From International Wealth Success, Inc., Bank Plaza, Merrick, NY 11566: *Business Capital Sources.* $15. 161 pg, 8.5 x 11 in. More than 1,500 lenders of real estate and/or business funds, listed by state. Updated every six months. Includes many ideas on how and where to raise money for business.

*2,500 Active Real Estate Lenders.* $25. Comprehensive listing by city and state of some 2,500 active real estate lenders who lend for one or more of a variety of real estate purposes, including mortgages of all types, construction, development, etc. 154 pg, 8.5 x 11 in.

*How To Borrow Your Way To Real Estate Riches,* by Tyler G. Hicks. $15. Lists hundreds of Government loan programs for income real estate of many types. States amounts available, qualifying requirements, etc. Loans and/or guarantees listed go as high as $40-million; duration as long as 40 years.

*Complete Guide To Local Money, Financing And Development Sources For Real Estate And Business.* $15, 50 pg, 8.5 x 11 in. Lists hundreds of development agencies throughout the United States which are seeking to encourage real estate and business growth. Many of these agencies can be helpful in securing financing for real estate and business projects.

*The Million-Dollar Guide To Real Estate Fast-Financing Shortcuts To Money And Capital For Your Projects.* $25, 145 pg, 8.5 x 11 in. Gives much data on hundreds of real estate lenders, some of whom make loan decisions (Go or No-go) in 24 or 48 hours. Most lenders are given a full-page description in this book.

*Comprehensive Financial Directory for Beginning and Experienced Wealth Builders in All Fields of Fortune Building,* $20, 100 pg, 8.5 x 11 in. Lists hundreds of money sources of all kinds for real estate and business. Includes underwriters who make stock offerings.

*Directory of Selected Housing, Land, Farm and Business Assistance Loan and Mortgage Programs in the Federal Government* $30, 236 pg, 8.5 x 11 in. Lists thousands of loan, mortgage, and similar programs in the Federal Government from which money in the form of loans or grants is available.

*Real Estate Fortune-Builder's Handy Guide to Unusual Money Ideas and Financing Techniques.* $10, 42 pg, 8.5 x 11 in. Gives data on publicly-assisted housing finance, loan interest calculations, and real estate investment trusts.

*SBIC Directory and Handbook of Small Business Finance,* $15, 135 pg, 8.5 x 11 in. Lists nearly 500 small Business Investment Companies and gives many hints on business finance.

Useful books giving many ideas on real estate financing but which do not—in general—contain specific names and addresses are:

Hoagland, H.E.—*Real Estate Finance*, $13.25, Irwin.

McMichael, S.L.—*How to Finance Real Estate*, $10, Prentice-Hall.

Steinberg, J.—*Mortgage Your Way to Wealth*, $8.95, Prentice-Hall.

Berman, D.S.—*How to Reap Profits in Local Real Estate Syndicates*, $19.50, Prentice-Hall.

Bohon, D.—*Complete Guide to Profitable Real Estate Leasing*, $8.95, Prentice-Hall.

Bockl, George—*How to Use Leverage to Make Money in Local Real Estate*, $7.95, Prentice-Hall.

Maisel, S.J.—*Financing Real Estate*, $9.95, McGraw-Hill.

Moser, L.E.—*How to Build a Fortune in Real Estate*, $7.95, Prentice-Hall.

Kent, R.W.—*How to Get Rich in Real Estate*, $7.95, Prentice-Hall.

### GET YOUR REAL ESTATE MONEY NOW

You now have—in the above money-source books—the names and addresses of more than 5,000 sources of real-estate and business money. Since real estate is a borrowed-money business, all you need do is:

1. Find the real estate you want
2. Get a price from the seller
3. Study the profit potential for *YOU*
4. Make an offer based on your study
5. Borrow the money *YOU* need
6. Go on to great wealth success
7. Expand your real estate holdings

### KNOW THE MAGIC OF REAL ESTATE

Many Beginning Wealth Builders (BWBs) overlook the real magic of OPM (Other People's Money) when they use it to purchase real estate. To help you understand exactly how you can go from pennies to millions in real estate in three years, I've expanded the above seven magic steps in Chapter 5 of this book.

When you've finished reading that chapter I'm sure you'll be willing to say: "Real estate is the best business known to BWBs anywhere!"

### Points to Remember

- Real estate is a borrowed-money business.
- More people probably borrow more money for real estate than for any other business.
- Beginners in real estate can usually borrow money for their deals almost as easily as experienced people.
- 100% financing of real estate (that is, taking over property without using any of your own money) is often possible.
- With thousands of real estate lenders in business today, you can usually find the real estate financing you seek.
- Real estate is a great business for BWBs.

# 4

# HOW TO AVOID BEGINNER'S
# MISTAKES IN REAL ESTATE

If you could sit with me at home in the evening for three or four nights while I answer phone calls from readers, I think you'd learn something about beginners' mistakes in real estate—and how *you* can avoid them. But my office is too small to accomodate all who would want to listen, so I'll have to tell you about those calls here in this book.

## SIX MISTAKES BEGINNERS MAKE

After listening to thousands of real estate beginner's proposals, I think I've been able to isolate the six most common mistakes beginners make. Here they are, in summary form. After you read the list, we'll discuss each mistake and show you why you should avoid it.

### Six Common Mistakes of Real Estate Beginners

1. Trying to buy—with 100% financing—a nearly new income property costing $1-million, or more, as the first property the BWB purchases.

2. **Trying** to buy—again as the first property and with 100% financing—a nearly new motel, hotel, or other type of short-residence facility.
3. Trying to buy raw land, which is non-income producing, without any cash available or cash to "carry" the land.
4. Mistaking a business—such as hog raising, rabbit culture, pig farming, etc.—for real estate.
5. Unwillingness to upgrade no-cash easy-to-get property to raise its income and value while increasing your wealth.
6. Denial of the basic real estate fact-of-life—that it takes time to make money in real estate.

Let's take a look at each of these mistakes. By reading about them *now,* I hope to be able to show *you* how to avoid these mistakes.

And by learning *now,* you will—I hope—be able to build your real estate riches faster and with fewer problems. So we're learning—in a positive way—how not to make real estate mistakes!

### BUY RIGHT FOR YOU—NOW

The calls come through to my office, week after week, month after month, year after year. Though the words differ a bit from reader to reader, the message is much the same:

> Ty, I've found this great, great income building! They're asking $2-million for it, with $500,000 down. It has every thing—pool, garage, security system, etc. And the income is nearly half a million a year! I don't have any cash but I'd sure love to get this building now. How can I get this property? And another thing, Ty. Time is of the essence—if I don't get the cash in the next three days, I'll lose out on this deal! You *must* help me get this money for the down payment—now!

I've heard this plea over and over—from one end of the world to another. Yet the calls keep coming, despite the fact that:

- The "debt service"—what you have to pay to pay off your loans—almost wipes out your profit on this type of building.
- Your chances of borrowing $500,000 with no cash in your pocket, no assets, sparse credit history, and little or no real business experience are practically nil!

- In real estate, when you start small, you have to build *reasonably* slowly. You can—I find—easily build from zero dollars to holdings of one million dollars in three years. To start with a property costing $1-million, or more, is difficult. I've seen it done a few times—but not too often.

## LEARN THE REAL NAME OF REAL ESTATE

The real name of real estate is *Time*. You must—when you have no cash to start with—build slowly. The way to go from zero cash to property worth $1-million in three years is—I have found:

- Start small with a building you can finance with 100% borrowed money
- Improve the value of this property by having it repaired and painted—if necessary
- Raise the rents to increase your income
- Show—on your financial statement—the results of your efforts—by increasing the value of the first property you purchased. (The increase you show could range from a low of 5% to a high of 30%).

So listen to me for a moment. You *might* be able to build holdings of $1-million in one year, or $2-million in 2 years, as some of my readers have. But the *usual* reader raises his or her worth by about $300,000 per year, starting with *no* cash.

Your best road to real estate wealth, starting with *no* cash, is the 36-month step sequence shown in a later chapter of this book. While *you* can easily exceed this schedule, let me say this:

> If you stick with me, I'll easily make you the proud owner of
> $1-million worth of real estate in three years, starting with no
> cash. Then—in your second three years—you can easily outpace
> my modest goals by two, three, five, or ten million dollars!

Yes, *good* friend, I *can* give *you* the lazy person's way to riches—if you're willing to put in three years of your *spare* time. And, while you're building *your* spare-time million-dollar fortune you can:

- Hold another job
- Run another business

- Travel, vacation, work, or play
- Build an empire in another field
- Do anything *legal* that pleases, amuses, or delights *you*

Just remember this fact—the second name of real estate is *TIME*. If you buy real estate at the *right* time—when prices are low—you can sell soon when prices are higher. But—if you buy when prices are high, and you have *time*—you will still make money! So my conclusion is this:

> There is probably no wrong time to buy well-located real estate—if you have time to wait for the price of your property to go up!

### SMALL STARTS MAKE BIG FORTUNES

In my wide travels through the real estate world I've met more millionaires who started small and grew big than I have those who started big and grew bigger. Here are a few of the small starters.

Floyd C. works for an airline as a ground supervisor. At his West Coast base airport, Floyd noticed that many of the young girl stewardesses didn't want to stay in the company-rented hotel rooms while off duty. Instead, these pretty young girls wanted to "stay in a place of their own." This gave Floyd an idea.

Why not take over one or more older buildings, have each converted to two or more apartments, and rent them out to the girls? Floyd did some research, asking the many girls who passed through his office each day what they thought. The response was an instant and delighted *yes*!

One other important point came out during Floyd's "research." About half the girls said: "Get a place near the airport." The other half of the girls said: "Get a place near the beach!' So Floyd decided to get two places—one near the airport and the other near the beach. Girls from either place could use the other place free.

So Floyd started looking for suitable houses to convert. He soon found that there were plenty of garden-apartment type buildings around $1-million, and up. But, after calling me, Floyd wisely decided that this type of building was *not* for him at the start because:

1. He had little cash—$200 to be exact
2. His chances of borrowing the needed down-payment (about $300,000) were slim
3. He'd be better off starting small and growing big

So Floyd took over two repossessed four-family houses for no cash down. He then quickly borrowed $7,500 on each house to have improvements made. Six weeks after taking over each building, Floyd had rented out all eight apartments with 5 girls in each at a monthly rental of $250 per apartment. Thus, Floyd's monthly income is 8 x $250 = $2,000.

Today, two years later, Floyd has ten houses near the airport and eight near the beach. His monthly income is over $40,000, giving him a yearly gross of over $500,000.

"Soon," Floyd says, "I'll take over a garden-type apartment house with 40 or 50 units in it. But when I do, I'll:

- Know what the building will need in the form of down payment, expense payments, etc.
- Make a profit from the very first day
- Be sure to build my wealth faster

Yes—you *can* make a million in real estate—starting with *no* cash. But the best way that I know of is to start small and grow big—fast. So take my advice and start on the least cash possible. If you do, you'll probably find I'm right—while you're making your million. I have nothing to sell you except your success!

## STAY AWAY FROM MOTELS AND HOTELS

Motels, hotels, and other short-residence buildings are *businesses* that sit on real estate. Thus, many motels and hotels get more income from their restaurant, bar, and catering facilities than they do from their rooms. So, unless you know the motel or hotel business well, stay away from both at the start. Why? Because motels and hotels:

- Are labor intensive—you need a big staff with high labor costs
- Many different skilled trades may be needed in a motel—cook, maid, bartender, night clerk, etc.

- A good motel or hotel location often has a much higher land cost or rental cost than can be justified by the business income for a beginner
- Land values seldom rise as fast for motels and hotels as for other real estate

So—unless you've had years of experience as a motel or hotel operator—stay away from these businesses as your first real estate investment. Later—after you've made big money in conventional apartments or commercial property—you can take on a motel or hotel, as a *business* deal. By that time your experience will guide you.

## BE CAREFUL OF RAW LAND DEALS

Many people dream of hitting the big money in raw land. "Buy good land in the path of development and hang onto it," these folks say. "When land use catches up with your piece of mother Earth, you'll make a bundle! All you need do is sit tight and wait."

It's so true, I sigh. But there's an enormous IF behind all raw land buys. This big IF can be summarized thus:

- *If* you have the money to put down on the land
- *If* you have the money to pay the taxes until you sell
- *If* you can wait for land use to catch up with you
- *If* you can sit on a no-income property for long enough

Land use moves outward from the central area of a city at the speed of about 1 mile per year, when the city is expanding. But:

- Not all cities are expanding
- Land values go up by different amounts, depending on location
- When you start with no cash you need a cash *producer*, not a cash "eater"

Sure—raw land *can* make you big money! But the time to speculate in raw land is *after* you make your million in income real estate. Then you can afford to:

- Wait until land values rise
- Pay taxes from other income
- Have a cash "eater" instead of a cash grower

Income real estate gives you two big plusses that are lacking from raw land—(1) cash flow, and (2) a tax shelter which allows you to keep more of your cash. And—if you have other income from sources different from real estate—you might be able to (1) reduce the over-all cost of borrowing money for business, and (2) shelter some of your other income from taxes. But all these advantages assume that your real estate "pays its freight"—that is, has a cash *income*. Raw land seldom has a cash income.

So, avoid raw land at the start of your real estate career. Later—after you're worth a million—you can get into all the raw-land deals that interest you!

## DON'T CONFUSE REAL ESTATE AND BUSINESS

In real estate you profit two ways:

1. From rental of space to your tenants
2. From the growth in value of the property you own and rent out

In business you profit in only *one* way—from the sale of the product or service which you are marketing. So real estate and business *are* different! This brings out an important fact:

> Unless the BWB sees the difference between real estate and business, he or she is likely to earn less money because most businesses allow you to earn money only one way.

Thus, hog raising, rabbit farms, and mink ranches are essentially businesses. True, the real estate they require may go up in value. But—like motels and hotels—you must be something else first, before you make the big money in real estate.

Ted C. learned this important fact when he bought a mink ranch. In buying the ranch, Ted thought he was getting into real estate in a big way. But Ted soon found that the ranch needed much more business skill and experience than he had.

"What can I do, Ty," he wailed over the phone one night. "I can't meet the monthly payments on the ranch because the business isn't giving me the cash flow I expected."

"What do you *really* want to be in?" I asked him "Real estate—not minks," he groaned. "Then get yourself a mink rancher—someone who understands the business—and let him run the ranch for you while you concentrate on the real estate deals." "I'll try," Ted said, sounding defeated and beaten.

I didn't hear from Ted for three months. Then one night the phone rang and it was Ted. "Ty," he said excitedly, "your methods really do work. I didn't believe you when you told me to get a rancher to run the ranch. But I figured I had nothing to lose. So I got the guy and put my time in on the real estate. In three months I've sold off half the ranch for a profit of sixty grand. And it looks like I can get ninety or a hundred grand for the other half! How does that grab you?"

"Great," I laughed. "You now see the difference between real estate and business." "I sure do. Thanks to you I'll make my million—in real estate," Ted said with a tone of gratitude in his voice.

So—if you want to make *your* fortune in real estate—keep the basic differences in mind. Then you'll have a much better chance of getting richer, sooner!

## MAKE MONEY FROM LOW-COST PROPERTY

"Ty," people often say when they call me in the evening about real estate, "I'm only interested in top-quality, high-cash-flow properties in a good part of town. I won't touch anything else."

"Great," I reply. "How much cash do you have to put into your real estate? '

"Well, that's my problem," most of these BWBs say, rather lamely. "I don't have any cash at all. So I'll need one-hundred percent financing. In fact, if I could get one-hundred and five or one-hundred and ten percent financing I could really swing the deal."

When I hear such remarks from people who:

• Have never made a dime in real estate
• Don't have any cash of their own

- Refuse to start small and grow big, and
- Fail to learn the facts of this business

I'm likely to explode. "Darn it," I say to them, "if you know so much about the place you want, why do you bother me?" And the usual answer is: "Because I don't know how to get the money I need. Won't you please help me, Ty?"

"Sure, I'll help you," I usually say. "But you'll have to do things *my* way. I'll bring you to the point where you're a millionaire in three years. After that, you're on your own."

"Okay," the reader usually replies. "How do I start?"

"You start," I say, "by going where the money is—namely to no- or low-down-payment buildings that can zoom your riches in just a few months."

"But what about the neighborhood," the reader next asks.

"Friend, I reply, a dollar of income from a no-down-payment house is the same as a dollar of income from a high-cost house. And what's more, the income dollar from low-cost property will probably be a much more profitable dollar to you because less of it will go for paying various expenses. By this I mean that you'll be able to spend, on yourself, 20¢ to 30¢ of the dollar you get from low-cost income property. But you'll be able to spend only 3¢ to 6¢ of the dollar you get from high-cost, newer housing."

So don't be afraid to start building your first million in the less attractive parts of town. Why? Because:

- You get more income for your money
- Properties can be taken over faster
- Many zero-cash deals are possible
- One-hundred percent—and better—financing is common
- Your spendable income is much higher
- Tenants are often more loyal
- Labor is easier to get
- Repairs and improvements will cost you less

Sure—there are problems with low-cost real estate. But you'll also have problems with high-cost real estate. So—unless you have a bundle of money you inherited from a rich relative, or won at the races, steer clear of high-cost income property at the start of your career. You'll make *your* first million much faster—if you take my advice!

## TIME IS REAL ESTATE

If you want to make a million dollars in six months, or less, don't get into real estate. Instead, go into a mass-market item like hula hoops, license-plate holders, washing-machine soaps, etc.

With a mass-market product you can either: (a) hit the big money fast, or (b) go broke in a few weeks. By contrast, in real estate, you can: (a) make a million in three years, with great certainty, (b) seldom lose your money if you pick reasonably well located income properties and wait for your rewards!

So you *must* be patient in real estate—there is just *no* substitute for time which:

- Pushes the value of your properties up
- Gives you rental income
- Helps reduce what you owe
- Provides you with experience
- Develops your judgment
- Gives you a tax shelter

If you're in a big hurry for riches, don't go into real estate. Instead, go into another business. You'll be much happier—and you may make big money faster. Then, again, you may not!

## PROFIT NOW FROM OTHERS' MISTAKES

You now know six common mistakes that real estate beginners make. Don't you make any of these mistakes! Why? Because, by using the advice in this book you can:

- Build a million-dollar real estate fortune in three years
- Go on to greater wealth
- Branch out to other businesses, if you wish

While there are other mistakes beginners make in real estate, the above six are probably the most common that I've seen. So avoid them whenever you can!

### Points to Remember

- Mistakes can hurt you in real estate—just as in any other business.
- Try to avoid buying nearly new property with 100% financing at the start of your real estate career.

- Recognize the difference between real estate and other businesses.
- Don't let non-income-producing raw land run you into heavy debt.
- Never be afraid to up-grade zero-cash property.
- Remember—always—the secret of real estate wealth success—*Time!*

# 5

# SEVEN LUCKY STEPS TO BECOMING
# A REAL ESTATE MILLIONAIRE

So many of my readers have made a million or more in real estate in three years, or less, that I'm positive I can show you how to do the same. And I'd like to give you—in this chapter—the seven lucky steps which I think can make *you* a real estate millionaire in 36 months, or sooner. Here are these seven lucky steps—written especially for you:

1. Get started with the *right* view of your future real estate wealth
2. Pick the way *you* want to make your real estate fortune
3. Find the financing sources you need, using the hints in this book
4. Look for the type of real estate that you've decided will make your fortune
5. Take over the real estate you want
6. Build the income and value of your property
7. Continue expanding your real estate empire until you reach your money goal

Now let's look at each of these seven lucky steps from *your* view. You'll soon see how you can make a real estate fortune in three years, starting with *no* cash.

## GET STARTED WITH THE RIGHT VIEW

Chapter 4 tells you how to avoid beginner's mistakes in real estate. Read that chapter again and again because it will help you keep the right view of real estate at all times. In quick, short bits of powerful money knowhow, this view is:

- Real estate is a business—you buy property for only one reason—to make money from it.
- You must *not* look at property as though you were going to live in it or use it—you must look at property from its income potential.
- Real estate is a borrowed-money business—so you must seek to put the least money possible into *every* property.
- You must know—in advance—the exact profit each property will pay *you*, based on your careful study of the properties you're considering.
- Once you take over a property, the next step is to raise its income to *you* because this gives you a bigger cash flow and a larger value for your property.
- Get started in your real estate fortune building with a plan that "points" you towards the amount of wealth you seek—$1-million, $10-million, $100-million.
- Learn now, and admit it here, that real estate is forever tied to time—without time real estate won't make you the big money you seek.
- Put yourself into your real estate, making your holdings *you* and you alone so your tenants recommend you and your properties to others.
- Save the money you make from your real estate and put it into more property until you reach your wealth goal.

To summarize these nine golden key ideas about your real estate future, you can say:

Real estate is a borrowed-money business in which fast income from property held for a number of years can easily make you a millionaire.

Also—get started right in your real estate wealth-building career and I guarantee you that great wealth will soon be yours.

Remember--I have nothing to sell you but your success! Here are two examples of how people got started right and hit the big money.

One of my East Coast readers, a young person with a growing family, took over 400 rental units in less than three years, using borrowed money. With an average rental of $150 a month, his yearly income, before expenses, is $720,000! Thus, he used the *borrowed money* aspect of real estate to the hilt. And a Western reader writes: "We, my wife and I, have been using the zero-cash approach to real estate for several years. Today we have 72 units and we are constantly looking for more. Our income is more than $100,000 a year." This, again, is an example of using the *borrowed-money* way to wealth in real estate!

## PICK THE WAY TO YOUR FORTUNE

There's just *one* fast, easy, sure way to *your* first real estate fortune—in my opinion—and that is through income property. Now I'm *not* saying that you must be in any special type of income property. But I am saying that:

> Income property can make you a millionaire. Non-income-producing property can break you.

The income property you pick can be of many types, such as:

- Apartment houses
- Townhouses
- Factories, warehouses
- Parking lots, auto wrecking yards
- Tennis courts, swimming pools
- Stores, shopping centers
- Hospitals, health clinics
- Office buildings
- Other

But no matter what type of property *you* pick, your cash income from the property *must* be greater than your expenses related to this same property. Always apply the acid test for real estate success invented by your author, Ty Hicks, namely:

To decide if real estate property will be profitable to you, ask
yourself the question: How much cash income from this property
can I spend each month on items other than the property?

The larger the amount of cash you have left each month, the
better—in general—will the property be for you. When you look at
the income summaries of various properties, you will often see
numbers such as these:

| | |
|---|---|
| Gross income: | $82,000 |
| Total expenses: | 84,000 |
| Income or (loss): | (2,000) |
| Amortization: | 10,000 |
| Net profit: | 8,000 |

At first glance it seems that this project is giving you $8,000 a
year in income. But it isn't! Instead, the "income" property is
*costing* you $2,000 a year in money you'll have to put into the
building to keep it going. Keep this important fact in mind at *all*
times:

You cannot spend amortization. So you must be able to "walk
away" with real cash at the end of each month.

To give a cash income, these figures should look like this:

| | |
|---|---|
| Gross income: | $82,000 |
| Total expenses, including | |
| amortization: | 68,000 |
| Net profit: | 14,000 |

So choose your projects carefully. Go into whatever type of real
estate interests you. Just be certain that the cash flow is high
enough to cover your vacancies. The usual vacancy rate used in
figuring an apartment-house income property is 5 percent. This
means that a property which is figured to yield $100,000 income
per year when fully rented will—for your planning purposes—be
figured to give you only 95 percent of this, or $95,000 income per
year.

Now let's see how other BWBs make money by picking the kind
of real estate that interests them. Here are two real-life incidents.

**Recreational Real Estate Pays Off**

Bert K. is a tennis "nut." He plays tennis day and night. I've even seen Bert "playing tennis" in his office while talking on the telephone. The way he does this is to bounce a ball off one wall in his office, using his tennis racquet, all the while talking on the phone. The horizontal dividing line between the lower paneling and the plaster upper portion of the walls forms his "net."

So Bert's natural desire—you might guess—is to own a tennis court. The only trouble is that Bert is a young (32-year old) family man with big responsibilities. So when he asked the seller for the price of a new indoor tennis building having four courts he was almost floored by the figure given him—$450,000, with $150,000 down. "There must be another way," Bert said to himself. (This "must-be-another or better way" is a trait of most BWBs I meet).

So Bert decided to see what other kinds of tennis courts he might buy, starting with no cash. He quickly found another kind—the inflatable building which is kept up by low pressure air being fed into it by a small air compressor. And though they might look flimsy, records show that these inflated buildings are seldom blown down and are almost never blown away in storms. Better yet, Bert found that he could rent a building and compressor, with *no* cash down. Now, all he needed was land.

Searching his local newspapers, Bert found two acres of land advertised for rent on the outskirts of town. But the land wasn't improved—that is, it did not have electrical, sewer, or water service. Fortunately, by using his head, Bert was able to work out a way of renting a portable generator, a water tank and two chemical rest rooms. To protect himself, Bert had an option-to-buy clause written into each rental lease. This clause allowed him to buy the building and equipment during the first year, getting full credit towards the purchase price for the rent he had paid.

To get some operating cash, Bert formed a tennis club, and sold 20 memberships in his tennis club for $1,000 each. With this money he had the land flattened and clay courts installed. Soon, other people joined the club, but their membership fees were $1,500 each because the club was about to open.

Four months after opening his club, Bert was taking in $3,500 a month in court rental fees. Six months later Bert bought the land, building, and equipment. Today Bert has six such tennis buildings in various locations. And already he has sold the land for five of the buildings and leased it back from the buyer. By doing this, Bert was able to convert his "land-heavy" position into a "cash-heavy" position, improving his financial condition. For, as Aristotle said: "Even happiness requires some external prosperity."

**Strings of Income Properties Pay Off**

Kathy L. works as a so-called "executive secretary," in a large firm. While the title may sound great, ":the job is nothing more than a glorified secretary's spot," Kathy says. "The pay is low, the hours are long, and the chances for moving ahead are nil. So why do I stay?" Kathy asks. "For just two reasons—my time is my own and I can come and go as I please. This allows me to spend time on my spare-time business during the day. And having a job that gives me an important-sounding title enables me to borrow money for my business. This is very important to me."

But getting money for her business wasn't always easy for Kathy. When she started in real estate, Kathy dreamt of a brand-new spotlessly clean 100-unit rental property on which she could borrow the down payment. Kathy soon got a rude shock when she learned that: (1) Many banks avoid lending money to women, thinking they are less reliable than men. (This is a narrow-minded view of half of our population!) (2) Borrowing a 100% down payment for a new, recently completed building is often difficult and expensive.

But Kathy didn't give up. "There must be a way around the discrimination and cost problems," she said to me on the phone one night. "There sure is," I replied. "Do the bankers a favor and take over some of their re-possessed properties. They'll forget your gender and will even pay your closing costs!"

So Kathy "lowered her sights," as she said, and decided to do the possible, instead of not doing the impossible. By visiting banks during early or late morning hours, Kathy found the bankers both interested in, and willing to, listen to her requests.

In just six months, Kathy took over a number of older buildings having a total of 300 rental units, with an average "talking" rental of $100 per month. Kathy's cash flow from non-job sources went from zero to $30,000 per month. Once she achieved this level, Kathy sat back for awhile to survey her business and rearrange her financing.

Another six months passed. During this time Kathy made many improvements in her buildings and was able to raise her cash flow to $45,000 per month. With such a cash flow and an impressive list of real estate holdings, Kathy easily borrowed the 100% down payment for the original building she wanted. Today her realty income holdings exceed $1-million.

What Kathy's experience brings out is: (1) You *must* not give up—you have to keep trying, (2) you *must* begin with the possible and go on from there to the "impossible." Why? Because when you start with *no* cash, it is difficult to "write your own ticket." Later, when you have the income *and* the assets, you can do what you want to do!

So you see, you *can* do what you want to do, in real estate. But you must pick a way to your real estate fortune which:

- Is possible for you
- Gives you instant income
- Fits in with your capital
- Can build your fortune fast

So—please—listen to me until you earn your first million in real estate! After that you can do as you please. You can even tell me how you'll make your second million!

## FIND THE FINANCING YOU NEED

Real estate is a borrowed-money business. By this I mean that most real estate deals are worked out on OPM—Other People's Money. This means that you can get started on zero cash—if you want to avoid putting any of your own cash into a deal. You can—if you wish—borrow real estate money from many sources, including:

- Commercial banks
- Savings and loan associations
- Insurance companies
- Mortgage lenders
- Savings banks
- Government sources

- State sources
- Second-mortgage lenders

If you want to learn some of the quickest ways to finance your real estate, I suggest that you do two things:

1. Continue reading this chapter carefully
2. Study the real estate financing course mentioned at the end of this section

Now let's look at *fast* financing methods for real estate. Why do I put emphasis on *fast* methods of financing? Because:

Fast financing of real estate is both possible and practical and allows you to build great riches sooner and with less delay.

### SEVEN METHODS FOR FAST FINANCING OF REAL ESTATE

Since many old-time real estate people are geared to a slow pace in their business activities, I've spent much time devising *fast* methods for you to get the real estate money you need. These fast methods are just as good as (or maybe even better than) the slow methods; further:

Fast financing helps BWBs in the area they usually find the most difficult—namely money. And these methods help quickly.

Since most BWBs who come to me are in a hurry, they welcome my fast financing methods. And even those BWBs who aren't in a hurry seem to welcome fast financing of their real estate fortune. Let's take a look at a number of these fast financing techniques here and now. Seven fast financing methods you can use quickly include:

- *100% financing* by taking over repossessions from banks, insurance companies, savings and loan associations is quick, easy, and painless. If you have a good credit rating you can—in some cases—be collecting income from your property in just three days. And your legal fees, real estate taxes, and escrow account will often be paid in full—in advance—when you take over the building. This saves you a bundle of cash.

- *Second-mortgage advance financing* can cut weeks off the time needed to take over a property. In this approach you arrange with a second-mortgage lender a tentative financing for a type of income property that you chose in Step 2, earlier. Thus, you might tell a second mortgage lender that you'll probably need a $75,000 to $100,000 second mortgage loan when you take over a property generating— let's say—$100,000 a year in income. You supply the facts about yourself which he needs and he gives his tentative approval of your loan application. Then—when you get the information on the property you want to buy—your loan can be approved quickly (in a day or two) if the property meets the requirements of your lender.
- *Setting up a "blind card" limited* partnership (LP) or real estate investment trust (REIT) before you find the *income* property you seek can give you the money you seek the *same* day you find the property! Actually, you can have your money long *before* you find the property you want because in a "blind card" LP or REIT you do not tell your investors exactly what types of properties you'll invest in until *after* you've invested their funds.
- *Sell stock* in your own real estate corporation before you take over any property. As an officer of the corporation (such as the president, vice-president, etc.) you are usually allowed to sell shares of stock without being a registered representative. This means you can build up a nice cash balance in your corporation, ready for investment in property when you find it.
- *Borrow from private or specialty lenders* you search out using your own ingenuity or the help of a publication such as *International Wealth Success,* the monthly newsletter of borrowing and wealth opportunities for both beginning and experienced wealth builders. This publication lists hundreds of little-known lenders every year.
- *Become a financial broker-finder-business broker* and find the money *you* need while being paid to look for and find money for *other* people. An excellent course showing you how to get started in this exciting profession is available at $99.50 from IWS Inc., at the address given elsewhere in this book.

- *Borrow or rent collateral*—such as stocks, bonds, letters of credit, leases, etc.—for the money you need *before* you need the money. To use this method, just estimate, *in advance,* how much money you'll need for your future real estate deals. Then rent the collateral you'll need. (Your banker will tell you how much collateral you will need for a loan of a given amount—say $200,000 or $400,000). Firms renting collateral are sometimes listed in the IWS newsletter mentioned above. Thus, in one recent issue an advertiser offered to rent high-grade municipal bonds (acceptable by almost any lender as collateral) for 3.5% a year. Thus, to rent a $10,000 bond would cost you $350 per year. This is a relatively low cost compared to the power you can get from fast financing of real estate using OPM (Other People's Money) backed by rental collateral!

There is a great potential for you as a financial broker in the real estate field. Thus, a reader recently wrote: "Thank you for IWS! Inside of the last 3 weeks I got a deal closed concerning construction financing . . . for a contractor. I made somewhat over $2-million ($2MM). Needless to say, I am still very happy over that accomplishment! Just thought that you would personally like to know this as this package came as a direct result of a connection made through IWS! . . . It is you that I have to thank most of all, due to the above-mentioned circumstance . . . Go! Go! Go! Never give up! Thank you sincerely, sir!"

Yes, you *can* find quick, zero-cash financing for the real estate you want. And you can often get this financing even though you have *no* cash to start with. Here are two living, breathing BWBs who did just that recently.

### Get Your Money First

Doug T. wanted to buy a 150-unit income apartment house but he had *no* cash. He went to his banker anyway and told him he'd like to buy the property which was fully rented, and on the outskirts of town.

"How much are you going to pay for the property?" the banker asked Doug. "I don't know yet," Doug replied. "Why don't you have it appraised and tell me what you'll lend me."

The bank appraised the building as worth $1.3-million. Doug figured this was 80% of what the bank thought the building was really worth, or $1.625-million. Also, he knew the bank would lend 80% of the appraised value, or $1.04-million. Knowing:

(a) What the property was worth, in the bank's opinion (that is, the apraised value), and

(b) How much the bank would lend him on the property,

Doug went to the owner of the property and offered him $800,000 cash as the total price of the building. The owner screamed, stamped his feet, threatened to cry—and sold out to Doug for $900,000, about 10% higher than Doug's offer.

Doug got his $1.04-million loan from the bank, paid the owner $900,000 cash and had $140,000 of *tax-free* cash left over. He had *mortgaged out* and had obtained almost 105% financing, starting with *no* cash. Yes, good friend, it *can* be done, *is* being done, and *you can* do it now, today, here!

**Cut Your Cash Needs**

BWBs who visit with me during lunch in midtown New York City, and those who read my many money books and my column in *International Wealth Success,* know that I'm a strong believer in quick education to increase your money-making ability. Now I'm not talking about four years of college. Instead, I'm talking about the many short, quick courses which cost little and might put millions into your pocket.

This is the kind of course I told Laura C. she should take when she told me she thought she could sell real estate in her spare time. Like most BWBs to whom I make suggestions, Laura resisted my idea that she take a short course and become a licensed real estate broker in her state. (Most BWBs I meet reject my ideas at first because the ideas are so simple and easy to use. Later on they use the ideas and are amazed that they work). That's what Laura did—she bought a good book, studied it carefully, took the exam, and received her license.

Laura didn't use her license for several years. But having the license never hurt Laura. And the annual fee was only a few dollars. (Do I hear you saying: "See the BWB *was* right; you had a bad idea."? If so, please read on).

The first chance Laura got to use her license was on a building she bought for herself. An office building came on the market, priced at $100,000 with $29,000 down. Laura had *no* cash at the time but she really wanted the building because it would clearly be a profitable takeover for her.

Laura asked the seller if she could act as the broker on the sale. He agreed and they signed a broker's agreement giving Laura a 6% commission, or $6,000 on the sale. This meant that if Laura bought the building she would need only $23,000 cash because the $6,000 commission could be deducted from the $29,000 cash down the owner was asking for the building.

Next, Laura had the building appraised by a bank and a mortgage company. The bank offered a $75,000 mortgage on its appraised value of $100,000. This meant that the bank would lend at 75% of its appraisal. But the mortgage company offered to lend 90% of the same $100,000 appraised value, for a loan of $90,000. Since the building would cost Laura only $94,000, that is, $100,000 less her $6,000 broker's fee, Laura had to come up with only $4,000 cash if she took the loan from the mortgage company.

Laura went back to the seller and asked him if he would give her a 5-year purchase-money mortgage for the $4,000. In this arrangement the seller accepts your promissory note in the form of a mortgage loan. The seller agreed because he wanted to sell fast and get out.

Laura closed the deal shortly thereafter, taking over the building with *no* cash down. So—once again—fast learning paid off for a BWB. Today, Laura's income from this building is over $12,000 a year. And, as Laura says, the building "runs itself."

For an excellent course on making big money from income property and vacant land of all kinds, you might want to order the *Real Estate Riches Course* from IWS, Inc., at the above address, for $99.50. A companion course that concentrates solely on real estate financing and loans is *Fast Financing of Real Estate Fortunes.* It is also priced at $99.50, from IWS, Inc.

### LOOK FOR YOUR REAL ESTATE

There are a number of ways of finding the real estate that will make you a millionaire. These ways include:

1. Large-city and local newspaper ads
2. Real estate magazine ads
3. Bulletins from local and national real estate brokers
4. Word-of-mouth ads from friends and associates

During your first few months of real estate wealth building, I suggest that you use *all* these methods of getting to know what's available, and where it's located. Why? Because, by using a number of different means to find what property is up for sale, you:

• Quickly get info on what's available
• Build a fast price knowhow
• Detect "lemons" that are being "shopped around"
• Find out typical cash-down needs
• Get to know people in the business

By looking for, and at, typical properties on the market, you will get a faster education than you ever thought possible. But in getting this education, you must keep an important fact in mind at all times, namely:

> There are high-cost properties and there are low-cost properties. If you look only at high-cost properties you will be overlooking many gems amongst the low-cost properties.

Put another way, a dollar you invest in a low cost property will often bring you much more income than the same dollar put into high-cost property. And the cash down payment you need for low-cost property is usually much less. This means:

> By starting with low-cost property, you can usually: (a) take over more property, (b) with less cash down, (c) while earning a higher income from the money you invest.

So start the right way to build your real estate fortune! Get lots of rental units to bring in lots of profit dollars. And you can help yourself get started quickly by looking in the above sources under the headings:

• Rental Property for Sale
• Apartment Houses for Sale
• Industrial Property for Sale
• Houses for Sale

Just remember to start off with something smaller than the Empire State Building, the Sears Tower, or the World Trade Center! Then you may wind up owning it some day! But whatever you do, *keep looking until you find the right property for yourself!*

## TAKE OVER THE REAL ESTATE YOU WANT

I've taken over or bought plenty of real estate in my business career. And I've worked with—and still work with—thousands of BWBs taking over real estate today. And the advice I give both myself and my BWBs always is:

> Have an attorney represent you in every real estate deal. Don't try to save pennies and wind up wasting dollars!

To take over real estate that can make *you* a profit:

1. Find the property; as described above
2. Decide what the property is worth to you
3. Make an offer *less* than the asking price using a suitable "pack" factor from Table I
4. Settle on a price
5. Reduce the down payment to zero, if possible
6. Get your attorney in on the deal
7. If you need cash, borrow it as shown elsewhere in this book
8. Have your attorney write a contract to buy the property
9. Meet with the owner and get the contract signed (have your attorney with you)
10. Finalize the financing, working with your attorney
11. Close on the property (your attorney *must* be with you at the closing)
12. Begin collecting *your* income

If you use the zero-cash methods I've told you about in this book, you can get the property you want without putting up any money of your own. And that—after all—is a good way to start. As I tell many BWBs—"Turn adversity into prosperity!"

## BUILD PROPERTY INCOME AND VALUE

The purpose of your real estate is to build a steady income for yourself of at least $100,000 a year. Sure, it's nice to stand in front of one of your properties and say: "I own that—it's all mine."

**Table 1: Typical "Pack" Percentages for Real Estate\***

| *Price of Property*<br>*(Land and Building(s))* | *Typical "Pack"*<br>*Percentage* |
| --- | --- |
| $    5,000 | 10% |
| 7,500 | 10 |
| 10,000 | 10 |
| 12,500 | 10 |
| 15,000 | 10 |
| 17,500 | 10 |
| 20,000 | 9 |
| 25,000 | 9 |
| 35,000 | 8 |
| 50,000 | 7 |
| 60,000 | 7 |
| 80,000 | 6 |
| 100,000 | 5 |
| 150,000 | 5 |
| 200,000 | 4 |
| 250,000 | 4 |
| 300,000 | 3 |
| 350,000 | 3 |
| 400,000 | 3 |
| 500,000 | 2 |

---

\**Note:* The percentage shown can vary from one area to another.

But if the property doesn't pay you the income you seek, then you may be less than proud. So aim at income—money is what will build *your* wealth faster than anything else!

To speed your income and wealth building, think in $100 or $150 units, depending on the going rent level in your area. Thus, you can quickly figure your monthly and yearly income before expenses by making up a short table like this, assuming 100% occupancy:

**My Real Estate Income**

| Number of Rental Units | Monthly Income | | Yearly Income Before Expenses | |
|---|---|---|---|---|
| | $100/mo | $150/mo | $100/mo | $150/mo |
| 10 | $ 1,000 | $ 1,500 | $ 12,000 | $ 18,000 |
| 15 | $ 1,500 | $ 2,250 | $ 18,000 | $ 27,000 |
| 20 | $ 2,000 | $ 3,000 | $ 24,000 | $ 36,000 |
| 25 | $ 2,500 | $ 3,750 | $ 30,000 | $ 45,000 |
| 30 | $ 3,000 | $ 4,500 | $ 36,000 | $ 54,000 |
| 40 | $ 4,000 | $ 6,000 | $ 48,000 | $ 72,000 |
| 50 | $ 5,000 | $ 7,500 | $ 60,000 | $ 90,000 |
| 75 | $ 7,500 | $ 11,250 | $ 90,000 | $ 120,000 |
| 100 | $ 10,000 | $ 15,000 | $ 120,000 | $ 180,000 |
| 1,000 | $100,000 | $150,000 | $1,200,000 | $1,800,000 |

So you see, when you get 100 or more income units, your dollar flow can get interesting--and lucrative! Here's a good example of that.

### Make a Million Helping Others

Jim T. always wanted to be rich. When we first talked, I told Jim: "Become a professional money maker in your own thinking first. Then pick a business in which you help others. Think of yourself as a professional and you won't go wrong!"

Jim had always wanted to own real estate. So--thinking of himself as a professional moneymaker--he took over a 50-unit building with *no* cash down because this gives a beginner the biggest leverage possible in local real estate. Since the property was a repossession in a depressed area, Jim knew he'd be helping people. And using a $100 unit as his base, Jim knew his income would be $5,000 a month, or $60,000 a year, before expenses and debt payoff.

Not having any cash on hand to fix up the building, Jim offered one month's free rent to each tenant who would fix up his own apartment. Most tenants agreed quickly to this fix-up plan. Within two months the value of the property zoomed and Jim was able to get a $10,000 building improvement loan to fix up the exterior. He also raised the rent of new incoming tenants to $150 a month.

Today, using this zero-cash approach to increasing the income and value of property, while helping people in depressed areas, Jim owns 3,000 apartment units, giving him a monthly income of $300,000, and a yearly income of $3,600,000! And he did this on zero cash, using the methods I suggest. You, too, can do the same—if you try!

## CONTINUE EXPANDING YOUR HOLDINGS

Set yourself a yearly money goal—such as a profit of $100,000 a year. Then set out to reach your goal in a year, or less.

Next, set a total worth goal—say $1-million. Choose a target date for reaching this goal—say 3 years from today. Then work at applying the methods I give you in this book. You, too, can easily become a real estate millionaire in three years, starting with *no* cash! And now here is one more method you can use—my Million-Dollar Real Estate Secret.

### MILLION-DOLLAR REAL ESTATE SECRET

Many real estate BWBs ask me how they can get started in real estate on zero cash. One little-known, secret way that I tell BWBs to explore is:

> Visit or call your local Apartment Owners Association and tell the person there that you're interested in taking over or buying some income property. Leave your name and address for use either on the bulletin board or in the Association's publication.

Now here's what will often happen.

Older apartment owners are often seeking to sell their buildings. But they frequently can't find a suitable buyer. So when you walk in seeking to buy, you are welcomed with open arms. And if you are a reliable and dependable person, you can often swing deals such as many other BWBs I know have, namely:

- Zero-cash down takeovers of valuable income properties
- 100% financing by private mortgage from the owner
- Valuable mortgage windfalls giving you cash in hand for buying a profitable property

- Free financing without credit checks, employment investigations, long applications, etc.
- A continuous supply of valuable leads on good properties for sale
- Friendships with people in the know in your local area

**Build Riches Thru Friendships**

In my travels about the world for business seminars, conferences, meetings, and various profitable deals, I've often noticed that many people are lonely. Tim K. found the same in his own "backyard" when he joined his local apartment owners association. Older members of the association whom Tim thought should be active, happy, and busy because they had 100 units ($15,000-per-month, $180,000-per-year income) were not. Instead, they were lonely, bitter, unhappy.

Tim, who was 32 years old at the time, decided to make friends with as many of these lonely people as he could. So he talked to many members of the association whenever he attended a meeting. To his delight, he found the lonely members ready and willing to talk. And as they talked, Tim could see some of the bitterness leave their faces. But what was more important, these people told Tim about their buildings and the problems they were having with them. So Tim found he was helping others while helping himself learn about properties!

Tim told several people about his situation. He was young, strong, ambitious, and anxious to own 50 or more income units. But he had no cash, collateral, credit, or cosigners. To Tim's delight, his new friends at the association became very sympathetic and wanted to either "mother" or "father" him, depending on the person to whom Tim was talking. In less than two weeks Tim had three offers to take over income units for no money down. He took over all three. Since the sellers gave him 100% financing, Tim put *no* money down, had *no* credit check, filled out *no* loan application! In 11 months Tim doubled his goal by taking over 100 units, giving him an income of $12,500 a month, before expenses. Today Tim is rapidly on his way towards becoming a real estate tycoon on zero cash!

You can put this million-dollar secret to work today. How? Just get in touch with your local real estate group and go on from there to join the property owner's association. Then—with a little time, dedication, and work—you're on your way to your first million in real estate—and probably in less than three years!

To find the address and telephone number of your nearby apartment owner's association, look in your phone book. You can also do the same for the real estate association. Or ask a local real estate broker for this information.

### Points to Remember

- Start fast with the *right* view of real estate.
- Pick—before you start—the way you want to make big money in real estate.
- Use ingenuity and reliable data to find the financing you need.
- Form the habit of regularly reading the real estate ads for the type of property you seek.
- Try to take over your income property for *no* cash down.
- Build the income and value of your property.
- Continue expanding your real estate holdings until you reach your wealth goal.

# 6

# TAKE THE RAW LAND
# ROUTE TO WEALTH

Raw land is usually *unimproved land,* that is, it does *not* have:

- Sewers
- Streets
- Lighting
- Curbs
- Water supply

or other improvements. Because nothing has been done to it, raw land is usually:

- Cheap
- Readily available
- Easy to buy
- Full of profit potential

But this is not all a song of plenty. Why? Because raw land:

- Pays you *no* income
- Can be a big tax burden

- May take years to develop
- Can be a drain on your income

"If all these drawbacks are true, why bother me with raw land?" you ask. Because, good friend, raw land—which you carefully select—can put you into the chips quickly and effortlessly. Let's see how.

## WHY RAW LAND IS VALUABLE

The major reason why raw land is valuable to people is:

Land is a limited-availability commodity because there is only a certain amount of land available and there is a growing demand for land everywhere.

Whenever you have a situation in which there is only a limited amount of a commodity available, and a growing demand for this commodity (such as land), the price of that commodity will rise. And the longer such a commodity is held, the higher (in general) will its price rise. So you can't lose on raw-land investments if you:

- Pick your land carefully, after you
- Analyze the direction of development
- Study the speed of development
- Wheel and deal for the lowest price

## ANALYZE THE DIRECTION OF DEVELOPMENT

Towns and cities usually grow in population as time passes. This growing population needs space—that is land. To satisfy the demand for more space, almost all communities expand horizontally. To expand horizontally, or on the flat, land must be developed, that is subdivided into:

- Lots, with
- Access roads and
- Side streets, having
- Sewers and
- Water supply and
- Electricity

If you can predict the probable direction of horizontal expansion of a town or city you can make big profits by:

- Buying raw land in the path of the community growth
- Holding the land until the growth reaches you
- Selling out to developers at a suitable price

Or you can, if you wish:

- Hold onto the land, instead of selling it
- Develop the land yourself
- Sell the developed raw land to builders

Or you can, if you wish:

- Go into the construction business and
- Build houses or other structures on your developed land

Thus, you can see that your potential is almost unlimited—*if you buy in the direction of growth.*

To analyze the direction of growth in an area you're considering, try the approach used by Saul C. to build a fortune in raw land. For each area you're considering:

1. Draw a map, such as Fig. 1, of the town or city and surrounding land, including the land you're considering. (Or you can use an Army Engineers' Survey map or a road map of the area.)
2. Read all the local papers, paying close attention to:

   - Housing-development ads
   - Shopping-center ads
   - Industrial-plant construction information
   - Any other items showing that people, or firms, are investing money in the area

3. Using a suitable symbol, plot each important item on your map.
4. Continue plotting these points until you think you see a direction of growth emerging, such as that shown in Fig. 1.
5. As soon as you see a direction of growth, buy land in the way of this growth. Buy the land at a distance from the community center which agrees with your analysis of the speed of development.

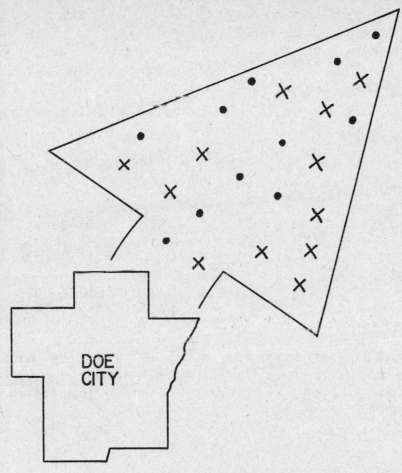

**Figure 1**

Mark the location of new stores, shopping centers,
and housing developments to learn expansion direction.

### FIND THE SPEED OF DEVELOPMENT

Saul C. kept a record of the speed of development on his map.
You can do the same and learn an enormous amount about your
area and the ways you can make money from it. Here's how.

1. Pick some measure of development—such as the purchase
of land for a shopping center
2. Enter on your map the date this event occurs

3. Keep adding dates to your map as you learn of each new event—such as the breaking of ground for a new factory
4. After you have six or more such dates, measure how far *out* from the center of the community the development moved with each date

Saul C. did this for the raw land in Figure 1 and came up with what he thought was a great discovery, namely that:

> Raw land is converted to developed land at the rate of about one mile per year in areas which are growing.

Only later did Saul C. learn that this "discovery" of his had been made by other real estate wheeler dealers in the past. Stated simply: *A growing city or town moves outwards in its direction of growth at the rate of about one mile a year.* Knowing this, and the direction of growth, you're ready to wheel and deal for your land.

### WHEEL AND DEAL YOUR WAY TO SUCCESS

What's a wheeler-dealer? How does he or she run a business? Why be a wheeler-dealer? Here are the answers to these basic questions. These answers could put a million dollars into your pocket in just a short time.

A *wheeler-dealer* is a businessman or woman who:

- Never pays the asking price
- Keeps his or her cash payments low
- Tries many alternate schemes
- Works business deals fast
- Develops unusual financing plans

The wheeler-dealer runs his or her business so that its:

- Costs are a minimum
- Profits arc the highest

Many wheeler-dealers run their business out of their hat—that is, they have no:

- Office
- Secretary
- Files
- Big investment

You should consider becoming a wheeler-dealer because you'll:

- Live more creatively
- Earn higher profits
- Get richer faster
- Have fewer worries

### LOW COSTS CAN MEAN BIG PROFITS FOR WHEELER-DEALERS

Here's an example of how a Beginning Wealth Builder (BWB) is using speed and good cost control to build a fast fortune as a wheeler-dealer.

In an issue of *International Wealth Success,* the newsletter for which I write a monthly column, I recently wrote on how big a business one person could run. Here's what one reader wrote in response to that column:

> Several months ago I read your book on building a business using *other people's* money.[1] I put some of the ideas to work and now have a very profitable business going.
>
> This morning I received your March issue of IWS and I read your page with interest as to how big a business one person can run. Let me tell you my experience.
>
> I devote about 75% of my time to this business and have a part-time office girl. In the four months I've been in this business my volume is already over $400,000. The only thing that is holding me back from doing $1,000,000 per month is the money to work with . . . . Thanks for the inspiration.

### HOW TO WHEEL AND DEAL IN RAW LAND

To wheel and deal in raw land you must:

1. Decide that you *will* be a wheeler-dealer
2. Use the methods of the wheeler-dealer, that is:

- Never pay the asking price
- Keep cash payments low
- Scheme your way to great success
- Work fast
- Be creative about financing

3. Keep thinking of new deals, new ways, new approaches at all times

---

[1] *How to Borrow Your Way to a Great Fortune*

Now I'd like to give you an example of a creative raw-land wheeler dealer. I've chosen him to tell you about because he used all the above approaches.

Cary D. wanted to invest in raw land in his area. But Cary had problems, namely:

- Very little cash—only $150
- No access to cheap land
- A miserable credit rating
- No source of loans

When Cary analyzed his situation and came to realize how badly off he was, he almost cried. But hope springs eternally in the heart of every BWB and Cary was no different from the others. "If I could only be more creative," he said to himself. So Cary decided to be more creative, by using my method called the Psychology of the Possible. It is based on the belief that: *Anything You Can Conceive You Can Achieve.*

### LIST YOUR MONEY NEEDS

Cary sat down and listed his money needs. If he were to wheel and deal in raw-land real estate he'd need:

- Cheap land
- A source of money
- An income

The land in his area was, Cary thought, over-priced. This meant he'd have to go outside his area. The realization that he'd have to go elsewhere was Cary's first step towards great wealth, but he didn't realize this at the time.

Looking around for somewhere to go, Cary glanced out of his window. To the east he saw some low hills—about 20 miles away. These hills were once the home of several mining towns. But the ore petered out and people left the towns for better digs elsewhere. As Cary stared at the hills, his eyes suddenly widened. There—in the hills—lay the answer to his raw-land dreams. Here's what Cary did.

### GIVE YOURSELF A MILLION-DOLLAR GIFT

Cary jumped into his car and raced to the hills. The first deserted town he came to had a weed-cluttered main street, a crumbling church, a dusty saloon, and a rotting mine-shaft housing. Cary dug around the old buildings until he found the name of the town.

Moving further into the hills, Cary did the same in three other towns. When he had all the information he could conveniently gather, Cary returned home.

The next day he visited his local library and did a quick research job on each of the four towns. To his amazement, and delight, two of the deserted mining digs were classified as cities. Now here's what Cary did within the next few weeks:

1. Asked his state government (by letter) for permission to restore one city
2. Elected himself mayor of that city
3. Prepared an offering circular offering municipal bonds for sale for restoration of the city, its land, and buildings

All Cary's steps were successful and he was able to restore the city as a tourist attraction. Further, he received a good salary as mayor from the proceeds of part of the bond sale. With this money he was able to take over some of the surrounding raw land. As the tourist business increased, Cary sold off part of his raw land at an excellent profit. He developed the remaining land to the point where it paid him an income. Today, three years later, Cary is a millionaire. Truly, he gave himself a million-dollar gift!

## BE MORE CREATIVE IN YOUR RAW LAND DEALS

Cary used great creativity in the land deal you just read about. You, too, can be creative in *your* raw land deals. Here are a few ways to be more creative:

1. Search for the unusual deal—such as the estate sale, land auctions, the unusable pieces of property.
2. Move further away from the city center but stay in the path of population expansion.
3. Be alert to industrial land buying by large firms—such buys almost always signal an upsurge in surrounding land values.
4. Jump onto the rocketing land values induced by a Disney World, a Six Flags Over Texas, etc.
5. Keep tuned to Government land offers—you can, at times, take over land for as little as $1 an acre.

6. Go foreign—to Canada, Nova Scotia, South America, Central America, the Carribbean, Europe, Africa. Land is land and if you get it cheap, it can do nothing but rise in value.
7. Check out wetlands (land under water). Bargains today can become "money machines" tomorrow.
8. Search out raw land with a good location—such as spectacular views, waterfront areas, lake sites, etc. Location *always* pays off—if it's good!
9. Explore the possibilities of "non-land" raw land, such as air rights over existing developed land—like railroad tracks, drainage tunnels, marinas, rivers, etc.
10. Watch for the growth of new towns, multiple-family housing developments, and similar projects in raw land areas. They signal big profits for holders of raw land further out.
11. List ways *you* can make *your* raw land more profitable. Consider any of these techniques—subdividing, developing to the point of streets and sewers, or actual construction of buildings.

## SPECULATE IN RAW LAND

When you speculate in raw land you will usually:

1. Take over land with the least cash
2. Hold the land for as short a time as possible
3. Sell the land for the highest price
4. Accept a long-term payoff for the balance

Let's take a look at how a speculator can make *BIG* profits with just a few dollars to start.

### Sell Before You Buy

To act as a real estate broker you must be licensed in most states. But you don't need a license to sell raw land on which you have an *option* to buy. Freddie L. uses the option technique to take over raw land with little cash down. And since raw land is cheap to start with, Freddie gets by on pennies. Let's see how.

Based on a study of the *direction* and *speed* of land development, Freddie takes a one-, two-, or three-year option to buy selected raw land. To get the option he pays the owner 0.5%, 1%, or 1.5% of the asking price of the land for the option. Thus, on a $10,000 raw-land property, Freddie would pay $50, $100, or $150, depending on how long he thought he'd have to hold the property before he could sell it. These sums are so nominal that most BWBs can raise them quickly.

Once Freddie has an option to buy a piece of raw land he has control of it until he either:

a. Sells the land
b. His option time expires

When his option expires without his having sold the land, Freddie either:

a. Renews the option, or
b. Loses his option payment

While loss of the option payment might annoy some BWBs, Freddie believes that the loss is small compared to the profit opportunity he has while he's holding the land, ready for sale. To sell "his" land Freddie:

1. Makes a list of its good features
2. Lists the potential uses for the land
3. Figures the type of customer (builder, developer, industry, etc.) for which the land is best suited
4. Prepares a mailing piece describing the land, the features, price, etc.
5. Mails the piece to potential buyers

Using this technique Freddie is able to sell over 95% of the raw land on which he takes options. And he *always* prices "his" raw land at twice its cost to him. Once he finds a buyer, all Freddie has to do is close the option deal, turn around and sell the land to his buyer. So, by combining raw land and mail selling, Freddie has made himself $500,000 in his spare time in five years—selling before he buys!

### Sell Lots for Future Homes

Tom Q. makes more than $100,000 a year selling raw-land lots for future homes. But instead of selling to the retiree on Social Security, Tom sells to:

    a. High-income executives
    b. Second-home enthusiasts
    c. Horse, cattle, and sheep grazers
    d. Housing developers

These people have the money to pay for well-located land which can:

• Go up in value
• Be developed
• Be used for grazing or other purposes

So Tom doesn't have to spend a lot of time trying to convince his prospects that well-located land has real potential. Instead, Tom aims at volume turnover to skyrocket his income and automatically build great wealth. How? Here's his technique.

Tom forms limited partnerships to take over thousands of acres of good land at a time. These limited partnerships are set up to produce the capital required for each block of land—the amount of money obtained from the limited partners can range from as little as $50,000 to as much as $1,000,000. "I got all the information I needed on limited partnerships from the IWS *'Starting Millionaire' Program*," Tom says. "This great course even includes the forms you need to set up such a partnership, using the guidance of your attorney."

Tom doesn't put up any money himself. Instead, he runs the partnership and gets a piece of the action—varying from a high of 20% on a $50,000 deal to a low of 5% on a $1-million deal. Now here's the procedure followed by Tom and his associates:

1. Locate suitable land
2. Draw up the limited partnership
3. Collect funds from sale of partnership units (similar to shares of stock)
4. Advertise the land after listing its features
5. Sell the land at a profit
6. Pay off the partners, or invest in other properties, depending on their wishes

Using this technique, Tom has built a neat fortune for himself in just a few years. Real estate is the basis of almost every fortune and it certainly is for Tom.

## DON'T LOSE MONEY ON RAW LAND

Raw land isn't all gold—you can get trapped into losing deals if you're not careful. Why is this possible? Because raw land:

- Pays you *no* income
- May have high taxes on it
- Can go down in value
- Sometimes is slow to rise in value

Now there are ways to get around most of these problems. The main problem, of course, is the lack of income from raw land, combined with the real estate taxes you might have to pay. To take care of the taxes, convert your raw land to a *taxpayer*—that is, property rented for business purposes temporarily to pay all, or most, of the real estate taxes on the property. Typical taxpayers you might consider renting your raw land for include:

- Parking lots
- Carnivals or fairs
- Tennis courts
- Above-ground swimming pools
- Athletic fields
- Temporary storage of large items

## MAKE TAXPAYERS PAY OFF FOR YOU

Two friends of mine own some waterfront raw land. This land is so far from nearby towns that it has been slow in developing. So taxes were a heavy burden on these wealth builders.

Craig, one of these friends, said to his partner, Bill: "We just have to get some money out of this land, Bill. If we don't, the taxes will 'kill' us." Bill agreed, but he didn't have any creative ideas.

When Craig came to me, I told him to analyze his land and then come up with a money-making idea. "Break down your investment into its elements, Craig," I said. "This will often help you decide what will make money for you."

Craig did as I advised, and quickly found that his waterfront land offered:

- Space—acres of it
- Flat terrain

- Millions of gallons of water in the bay on which the land bordered
- Easy access by a wide road
- Electric power outlets

Turning these facts over in his mind, Craig decided that a tenant needing space on level land adjoining water was his best prospect. With this "service" in mind, Craig made a list of prospective tax-paying tenants, such as:

- Boat storage for builders, marinas
- Heavy machinery storage
- Truck storage

As he wrote the last two words in his list, "lightning" struck. Just a mile from his land was a large fire-engine factory. This factory tested its finished fire engines in their rear yard by spraying streams of water into the air. Nearby residents were constantly complaining about the noise of the engines and the wind-carried spray from the nozzles. Craig's land would, he thought, make an ideal test area for the fire engines.

### MOVE FAST ON LAND IDEAS

Craig called the president of the fire-engine builder immediately and told him about the land, stressing its level layout, easy access, and unlimited water supply. The company president promised to visit the land the next day.

Craig and Bill were on hand when the president arrived to inspect the land. Within minutes Craig explained his idea to the company president. Together with Bill, he pointed out the good features of the land for fire-engine testing. There was:

- Easy drive-in access
- Plenty of flat parking surface
- Unlimited water
- No nearby complaining neighbors

The fire-engine firm president agreed to lease the land at twice the annual payments Craig and Bill were making for taxes, interest, and the mortgage. Today these two land speculators are sitting pretty as they collect a sizable income from their formerly "useless" land.

### USE THE POSITIVE FORCES OF RAW LAND

Many beginning wealth builders overlook the great advantages that raw land offers them, including the:

- *Time factor*—time works *with* you in raw land, instead of against you, as in many other investments. For instance, many raw land parcels will double in value in five years.
- *Population demands*—with a rising population, in certain areas, greater demands for raw land are being made every year.
- *More leisure time*—with the shorter work week, more people are seeking second homes, vacation retreats, and snug hideaways. Raw land is the main satisfier of these drives.
- *Limited supply*—"our Maker ain't makin' no more land for us," a poor farmer once said to me. "That's why I'm holdin' onto the back forty—may make some dough from them acres, someday." And sure enough, a year later he sold out for $80,000—more money than he'd earned in the last 10 years.
- *Enormous creative possibilities*—for making big money from the land while you wait for its value to rise. For instance, by converting the raw land to farming use you can collect *big* subsidies—often as much as $200,000 a year for either:

    1. Growing certain crops, or
    2. *Not* growing certain crops

Thus, you win whether you grow them or don't grow them!

- *Chances for big leases to large firms*—such as leasing corner highway properties to oil companies for gas stations. (The biggest leasing deal in history is that for the United States' embassy in London, England. The owner leased the land on which the embassy is built to the U.S. for 999 years! Top that deal, if you can.)
- *Exploration for natural resources*—can help reduce your income taxes on income from other activities. Thus, raw land may contain oil, gold, copper, uranium, silver, mercury, etc. You can take a *depletion allowance* when your

land produces certain of these minerals or petroleum. This depletion allowance helps you shelter some of the profits from your land's resources.

- *Temporary hobby use*—such as horseback riding, model-airplane flying, tennis, baseball, etc.—can turn a "loss-leader" property into a real winner. Your land pays you income while it doubles in value every seven years, or less.

## GIVE YOURSELF A MILLION-DOLLAR FORTUNE

Raw land can be *your* key to:

- Greater wealth
- A happier life
- Fewer problems
- More spending money
- Fast growth of your money

This chapter gives you ideas that can get you started in raw land, here and now. Throughout the rest of this book we'll point out other ideas you can use to make raw land your million-dollar money machine. So keep alert because there's gold waiting for you in raw land—if you're willing to go after it. As a final example to prove my point in this chapter, I'd like to show you how you can get the cheapest land on earth for no more than a few gallons of gasoline, a stimulating summer vacation, and a minimum charge.

### HOW, AND WHERE, TO GET RAW LAND UNDER $3 AN ACRE

Many people criticize the U.S. Government. But to me, our Government is the greatest in the world! And, friend, I've been around this world of ours plenty of times.

For instance, the Federal Government holds more than 750 *million* acres of land in the Western states. To claim some of this land, all you need do is load up your car with some 2 x 4 stakes, drive to a piece of federal land you think contains minerals, and hammer in the stakes at the boundaries of the piece you want. Then you register your claim in a local state office and, essentially, the land is yours!

Should you want full title to the land, you:

1. Apply for a *patent*
2. Prove there are some minerals on the land
3. Pay $2.50 *per acre* for the land (at the time of this writing)

When you get your patent from the Government, you don't have to develop the minerals. You own the land and you can sell it, develop it, hold it, or do anything else legal on the land. At $2.50 an acre (the price at the time of this writing), you're getting raw land at a cost of only about 0.005 *cents* a square foot, or you get about 200 square feet of land for *one cent*! Can you beat that deal in any other business? I don't think you can! Now, in our next chapter, we will take a look at another profitable aspect of real estate—residential properties.

### Points to Remember

- Raw land is valuable because its supply is limited.
- To make money from raw land, buy in the direction of growth.
- City areas often grow from their center at the rate of about one mile per year.
- You can wheel and deal in raw land and make a fortune.
- Being creative pays off in raw land deals.
- Be careful to make *all* raw land pay for itself.
- Some of the biggest bargains around today are in raw land.

# 7

## MAKE RESIDENTIAL PROPERTIES YOUR WEALTH SOURCE

Every human being in this world has two basic needs:

- Food
- Shelter

Without food we can't exist. But once we have food the next greatest need is a roof over our heads. Supplying this roof for a number of people can make you richer than you ever thought possible in just a few years. Let's see how.

### WHERE THE MONEY IS IN RENTAL PROPERTY

Good, well-located rental property is always in demand by:

1. Young marrieds
2. Singles
3. Older, childless couples (often called "empty nesters")
4. Non home owners

True, the demand for apartments may change from year to year. But, as a rental property owner of long standing, my income records and experience show that:

- Rental properties *are* safe investments
- Little management time is needed for them
- Your income is a steady cash flow
- There are plenty of zero cash, 100% financing deals around
- Income property is ideal for most BWBs

In rental income property you can own a variety of types of buildings such as:

- Luxury apartment houses
- Older, middle-class buildings
- Inner-city housing
- Single-family houses

Now most beginning wealth builders (BWBs) think that shiny new apartment houses are the answer to getting rich fast in real estate. Could be. But plenty of rich BWBs wouldn't agree with this. Talk to these BWBs and they'll tell you that:

The biggest real estate fortunes built by beginners are in the older, lower-down-payment buildings which stay fully rented at moderate to high rents.

Further, you can often take over old buildings with *NO CASH DOWN,* provided you are willing to assume—that is, make—the mortgage payments. Remember this fact about older buildings:

No lender wants to foreclose (take back) a building because his business is the lending of money—not the operation of buildings.

So you can easily get no-down-payment buildings which will produce good, spendable income for you. We'll soon show you exactly how to build your real-estate riches—starting with either some capital (money), or *no* money.

## HOW TO GET STARTED IN INCOME PROPERTIES

To get your *fast* start as a real estate empire builder, take these seven lucky steps:

1. Decide what type of property you'd like to own
2. Calculate how much money you can invest
3. Look for property of the type you want
4. Wheel and deal for your property

5. Close the deal
6. Start operating your property
7. Expand your property holdings

Now let's take a quick look at each step to learn how you can make real estate millions yours in the shortest time possible.

## DECIDE WHAT TYPE OF PROPERTY YOU WANT

In residential income property you can choose from among:

- New single-family houses
- Old single-family houses
- New multiple-family buildings
- Old multiple-family buildings

We'll take a look at each type to see which is best suited for your fortune building. Perhaps you'd be best off with a combination of units.

### Single-Family Houses Build Wealth

Single-family houses have strong advantages and disadvantages for your wealth building. The advantages are:

- Many single-family houses are available for *no cash down*
- Lower maintenance costs
- Fewer tenant problems
- Smaller building cost
- *No* heating bills
- Lower land taxes

Against these advantages you have to balance the disadvantages of single-family houses, namely:

- You're either fully rented (one family) or fully vacant
- When fully vacant, you have to make house payments out of your other income
- Tenants may not stay as long in single-family buildings as in multiple-family properties

Is there a way of avoiding the disadvantages of single-family rental housing? Yes, there is! "What's the way," you ask, sensing that I may have your answer to building a fortune in real estate in three years. Here's the answer.

To make big money in single-family houses, take over a "string" of them—say ten—with no cash down. Then operate them as a "horizontal" apartment house.

Tim K. did just this, taking over 12 single-family houses in four months with *no cash down.* Here's what his profit and loss statement looks like:

| | |
|---|---:|
| Monthly rental income = 12 houses x $350 per month each | = $4,200 |
| Annual rental income = 12 months x $4,200 per month | = $50,400 |
| Annual mortgage interest, and tax payments = 12 houses x $2,500 per house | = $30,000 |
| Annual gross profit | = $20,400 |
| Annual maintenance cost @ $200 per house x 12 houses | = $2,400 |
| Annual net profit | = $18,000 |
| Tax shelter from interest, depreciation, and repairs | = $16,800 |
| Taxable income | = $1,200 |
| Annual equity (or ownership) buildup | = $3,600 |

Tim saved the $18,000 income he received during his first year of owning these houses and used it as a reserve fund to cover unexpected vacancies, emergency repairs, and similar expenses. At the same time he took over 24 more single-family houses, giving him a total net income of a little over $55,000 a year—without having invested a cent of his own!

In any of the heavily populated areas of the United States, you can easily take over 36 such homes a year, giving you a total income potential of $162,000 a year at the start of the fourth year! And if you use the collateral provided by the houses and land, you can:

- Get tax-free second-mortgage loans
- Take over other types of property
- Raise your income *each* month
- Use home-improvement loans to improve your property

### HOW TO TAKE OVER SINGLE-FAMILY UNITS

To make one million dollars in real estate in three years starting with no cash by investing in single-family units:

1. Look for *resales* or *repossessions* in the real estate ads of your newspapers
2. Check out the cash needed—some of the ads will say *no cash down*
3. Try to find FHA and bank resales and repossessions—many have *no* legal fees, either

Once you locate one or more such houses, inspect them. Look for major defects, such as:

- Leaky roof
- Cracked foundations
- Flooded basements
- Broken beams
- Defective heating system

Don't worry about minor defects—you can get your tenants to:

- Repair broken windows
- Paint the inside or outside of the house
- Fix minor leaks
- Trim the grass, hedges, etc.

Now here's a valuable tip you can keep in mind whenever you are working out a deal for a no-down payment house:

Buy the materials and supplies (lumber, paint, etc.) for your tenants and they'll do most of the minor repairs the house needs while paying off the house for you and giving you a profit in the form of income and tax savings!

For best results, *always* have an attorney on hand when you take over *any* real estate. In some repossessions the attorney may be furnished you free of charge by the:

- Bank
- Mortgage firm
- Government agency
- Seller

If you're short of cash and have to pay the attorney (which you *won't* have to do often), get the attorney to agree to allow you to pay him out of the rent you receive. This will delay your payment and save you from having to put up any cash.

Yes, you *can* make *Big* money from single-family houses. Just be sure to:

- Take over with *no* cash down
- Aim for *volume* income
- Get your tenants to do work on the house
- Have an attorney at your side

## BUILD A FORTUNE IN MULTIPLE DWELLINGS

A *multiple dwelling* is any building having two, or more, families. Two-family units are also called duplexes; three-family, triplexes, etc. But when real estate people talk about multiple-family buildings they're usually talking about 20-, 30-, 50-, or even 300-unit buildings.

Let me—for a moment—show you the arithmetic of multiple units. Suppose that you have 1,000 rental units in 20 buildings. (This is easy because all you need is 20 buildings each having 50 apartments. This gives you a total of [20 buildings] x [50 apartments] = 1,000 apartments.)

Now if the *average* rent per apartment is $100 a month (which is a *low* rent today), your monthly gross income will be ($100 per apartment) (1,000 apartments) = $100,000. In a year you'll take in ($100,000 per month (12 months) = $1,200,000. And, friend, it's easy to take over buildings having 1,000, or more, apartments—if you're willing to work hard at your real estate business! (One real estate fortune builder I know of has 7,000 such apartments!)

The real beauty of the multiple-family building can be summed up for you thus:

- You can start with zero cash
- Competition is modest
- Pressures are few
- Cash comes in *every* month
- You have big tax advantages
- Inflation improves your investment and income
- You don't have to work 8-hour days—4 hours are enough
- You have an unlimited world for expansion—if you want to take on a large number of buildings
- Lastly—you get rich while you sleep because your properties earn money every minute of the day and night!

## HOW TO MAKE A FORTUNE WITH ZERO INVESTMENTS

Each year I talk to thousands of BWBs. While they differ in age, color, sex, religion, education, and ability, almost every one of these BWBs has the same basic problem, namely:

> Almost all BWBs lack start-up money. Ideas, energy, get-up and go, they have. But money to start a business is almost non-existent.

This is why I want to show you every possible way I know of to make a million dollars in real estate starting with zero capital.

You can get good, solid, profitable rental multiple-dwelling buildings in large cities anywhere if you look for properties which are:

- In changing neighborhoods
- Abandoned by owners
- Being "carried" by the city or state
- Being "carried" by banks
- Being "carried" by mortgage lenders

You can get any number of good buildings from such sources just by making a phone call or a short visit. Once you take over the building, with *no* cash down, you are on your way to your first million dollars in real estate.

"But why will they let me take over a good building with no cash down," you ask. "Good question," I reply.

Learn this fact of real estate life here and now:

> No bank, mortgage lender, city or state, wants to be in the business of operating a building if their major purpose in life is something else—as it usually is.

So when a bank, mortgage lender, city, or state, is "given" a building because the owner can't pay for it, the first step the organization takes is to look for someone to take the building off their hands. That someone could be *you*!

To make a fortune in real estate with *Zero* investment, take these tried and proven steps:

1. Locate one or more suitable buildings by using your local large-city newspaper, the monthly newsletter *International*

*Wealth Success,* or other suitable publications—such as those listed in the *IWS "Starting Millionaire" Program.*
2. Inspect the building
3. Offer to take over the building if it appears to be sound and rentable
4. Once you have possession of the building take steps to find any additional tenants needed
5. Collect a suitable rent security—one to three months' rent from each tenant if the former owner had no rent security
6. Take over the rent security from the present tenants in the building if the security is held by the seller
7. Arrange for all future rents to be paid to you by mail
8. Have any needed repairs made to the building
9. Scout around for the next building to take over

## COLLECT CASH FROM THIN AIR

Mel T. had a common BWB problem—no cash. He tried all sorts of lenders but his poor credit history prevented him from getting the loan he needed. Reading his local large-city newspaper, he saw several ads for no-cash down buildings. Since one of the buildings was in his neighborhood, Mel decided to check it out. To his amazement this sturdy, if old, building:

- Was 100% rented
- Contained 150 apartments
- Had $45,000 in rent security on deposit
- Was available for *no cash*
- Could be had by just signing a few papers
- Did *not* require a credit check

After checking out the building, Mel went home almost reeling with joy. Here was a gold-mine of cash (the rent security account would put $45,000 into *his* bank in his security-account name—more money than he ever had in his life before). Yet he felt full of fear. Questions ran through his mind:

- What if something went wrong with the building?
- Suppose all the tenants moved out?
- Would the taxes go up?
- Could the tenants stop paying rent?

## STOP WORRYING AND START ACTING

Mel called me at home, full of joy and fear. The rent security, which would become his as soon as he took over the building, attracted him like a magnet. But the imagined problems repelled him. "Ty, I don't know what to do," Mel moaned over the phone after calling me at home. "I'm so scared I think I'll pass out."

"Mel," I said, "stop worrying and start acting! Worrying won't get you anywhere—taking action will put *big* money into your empty pockets!" Then I analyzed the building and outlined the chances open to him. Here's what I told Mel:

1. With 150 apartments at an average rental of $100 per month, the monthly income would be $15,000; the annual income $180,000.
2. The $45,000 rent security could—in some states—be used as a compensating balance for a loan of five times that amount, or $225,000, provided Mel paid his tenants interest on their rent security (a legal requirement in some states). And—if he was lucky—Mel might be able to borrow as much as ten times $45,000 from a "hungry" bank!
3. He could get a $180,000-per-year income and $45,000 cash without a credit investigation. And, stretching a point a bit, I told Mel that this was probably the *only* way he could get money without having his credit checked.

Now, regarding Mel's worry about the building, this is what I told him—and these facts apply to all multiple-family residential buildings:

1. Every building has something "wrong" with it. But in older buildings the "wrongness" was usually corrected long ago. So really very, very little can go wrong with such a building!
2. Few buildings are ever vacated 100% by their tenants if the buildings are well kept, warmly heated, and repaired when necessary. It is usually easy to maintain the 80% occupancy which is needed to break even (that is, pay all expenses in such a building).
3. Real estate taxes almost always go up. To take care of this, you just put a clause in each lease, allowing you to raise rents when the taxes go up a certain amount.

4. Tenants *can* stop paying rent. But they won't—if you keep a clean, neat, warm building, no matter how old the building may be.

I must have convinced Mel (and I hope you) because the next day he called a lawyer and took the action he should have taken namely the signing of the agreement to buy the building.

Within a month Mel had full title to the building and—for the first time in his life—$45,000 in *his* bank account. Using this as a base of his real estate empire, Mel soon expanded to a million-dollar real estate empire. You can do the same, provided you:

- Are willing to work hard
- Are ready to search out no-cash deals
- Get good legal advice
- Keep expanding your ownership
- Raise rents when necessary
- Take good care of your buildings
- Forget your fear of the unknown

## USE OPM TO TAKE OVER PROPERTY

You may not like the kinds of buildings you can get on zero cash. Or there may not be any such buildings available in your area. So, if you still want to go into rental property, you'll have to put up some cash to take over one or more buildings. And if you don't have this cash you'll have to use OPM—Other People's Money.

In rental real estate OPM can take several forms, such as:

1. A purchase-money (PM) mortgage
2. A personal loan for the down payment
3. A business loan for the down payment
4. Mortgaging out with 100%, or better, financing—also called a windfall

Let's take a look at each form of OPM to see how you can use it to build your real estate empire.

## GET THE SELLER TO HELP YOU BUY

Many sellers of real estate are anxious to sell their property. Why? For hundreds of reasons, including:

- They're fed up with tenant complaints
- They don't want to run property they inherited from a deceased relative
- They're too old to stay in real estate
- They want to move south, west, north, east, up, down
- They want to get out of real estate and go into the stock market, the hotel business, or some other business

When you find a seller who wants out, you're in an ideal position to get the seller to *help you* buy his property. How?

By having the seller give you a purchase money (PM) mortgage—that is, the seller lends you the cash you need to buy the property.

Let's see how you can use this method right in your own city or town.

### Build Wealth With No Cash

Let's say you find a ten-year-old 50-family building that's for sale for $750,000, with a $150,000 cash down payment. The seller is the estate of the former owner of the building. After seeing an ad for the building in the newspaper you call the attorney representing the estate. You tell him of your interest in the building and he takes you on a tour of it.

You like what you see, and ask for the figures on the building. Here's what they show:

**Fig. 1**

| | | |
|---|---|---|
| Annual income | | $170,000 |
| Annual expenses | 30,000 | |
| First mortgage payments ($600,000 for 30 yr) | 50,000 | |
| Real-estate taxes, fees, etc. | 28,000 | |
| Total annual expenses | | 108,000 |
| Annual cash flow | | 62,000 |

"I don't have $150,000 cash," you tell the attorney. "But I'd be glad to take the building off your hands if you'll give me a 5-year PM mortgage."

"We wouldn't let this building go for no cash," he snorts. "It's too valuable a piece of property."

"It's valuable," you reply. "But here's my business card, just in case you change your mind. I hope to hear from you soon."

Now here's what you're figuring. The building statement shows an annual cash flow of $62,000 say $60,000 for talking purposes. You plan to pay off the $150,000 PM mortgage in 5 years and will offer the seller 10% interest. This means your PM mortgage payment will run about $45,000 per year, leaving you $17,000 cash per year for taking over a beautiful piece of income property.

Nothing happens for five weeks and you start to feel depressed. Then, late one evening, the phone rings. It's the attorney. "We're ready to talk about a no-cash deal—if you're still interested," he says.

Your heart jumps because you know that you have him where you want him "I'm busy the rest of this week," you tell him. "I'll call you next week to make an appointment (you need the time to contact your attorney and to make plans for working out the shrewdest deal possible).

A month later you own the building—without putting up a dime. You had to pay a slightly higher interest rate— 11%—than you expected. But you're still doing well. And since you expect to raise the rents soon, your cash flow will increase to a level where it is more than your higher interest cost.

## MAKE A MILLION IN THREE YEARS ON ZERO CASH

Assuming that you're willing to wheel and deal the way we just described, here's how *you* can make a million dollars in real estate in three years, starting with zero cash. I'll give you this well proven, nearly foolproof method in nine easy steps.

1. Pick the area in which you want to operate. (Large cities are usually best).
2. Locate your first building, as detailed above.
3. Buy the building using zero cash.
4. Give yourself two months to get the building in good working order.
5. Locate a second suitable no-cash building.

6. Use your first building as an asset on your financial statement when applying for a loan on the second building.
7. Assign a value to your first-building asset which—in your opinion—reflects the increase in value of the building resulting from your present and planned improvement of the condition and income of the building, and the effect of inflation. Thus, the value of your building could—in *your* opinion—rise 5% to 10% in three months.
8. Take over the second building with no cash down.
9. Repeat this process until you have made your million dollars.

Now what's the key secret to this Million Dollar Method (MDM)? The key secret is this:

> Using the MDM, you raise your assets from a small amount to a large amount without putting up any money of your own.

### THE MDM AT WORK FOR YOU

Let's see how the MDM might work for you, starting with the building you considered above. You'll recall that you "paid" $750,000 for the building. You "pay" the following amounts for the apartment buildings you buy over a three-year period:

| Building No. | Price You "Pay" |
|:---:|:---:|
| 1 | $ 750,000 |
| 2 | 500,000 |
| 3 | 360,000 |
| 4 | 825,000 |
| 5 | 435,000 |
| 6 | 200,000 |
| 7 | 908,000 |
| 8 | 452,000 |
| 9 | 155,000 |
| 10 | 875,000 |
| Total investment | $5,460,000 |

Thus, in three years you buy 10 buildings, "paying" almost $5.5-million for them. Yet, if you pick the buildings right, you won't have to put a penny down on these buildings. Now let's see what happened to your net worth in this time:

| | |
|---|---|
| Your real estate net worth at start | = $0 (we've assumed this) |
| Investment in holdings at end | = 5,460,000 |
| Appreciated value of holdings | = 6,000,000 |
| Equity increase of holdings—what you paid off on mortgages | = $ 400,000 |
| Spendable income from holdings during 3 years | = 300,000 |

So, your net worth rose as follows, during the three years:

| | |
|---|---|
| Spendable income | = $ 300,000 |
| Equity increase | = 400,000 |
| Property value increase | = 540,000 |
| Total net worth increase | = $1,240,000 |

You have thus made yourself $1,240,000 in three years—all on borrowed money! Let's take a closer look at each part of your new fortune.

### KNOW WHAT MAKES YOUR FORTUNE

You are now about to learn the inside facts on making your fortune in real estate without putting up a penny of your own. Please read the following words carefully—for *your* sake—not mine. Your Million Dollar Method made you a millionaire in three years by giving you:

- *Spendable income* of $300,000 from the rents you collected from tenants. This spendable income is Money-In-Fist (MIF) because it is what *you* have left after you pay ALL bills—such as repairs, taxes, light, heat, and mortgages.

- *Equity increase* is the amount of the mortgages you have paid off during the three years. Were you to turn around and sell all the buildings at exactly the *same* price as you "paid" for them, you would walk away with $400,000 in cash. And this equity increases has *ALL* been paid for by the loyal tenants of your buildings in their monthly rent payments to you!

- *Property value increases* of $540,000 result from the steady appreciation of property prices throughout the world. The property-value increase is the amount of profit you would earn if you sold your buildings at the end of three years of holding them.

So you see, you *can* make a million dollars today, using borrowed money. All you need do is put the MDM into action today!

## BEWARE OF WEALTH-BUILDING PROBLEMS

When you use the MDM you are almost certain to run into problems. Why? Because when you get income-producing property with no money down, you are usually dealing with buildings which:

- Are in changing areas
- Have tenants who often move
- May have serious maintenance needs

So don't say I didn't tell you! But let me also say this about the MDM:

Everyone who has ever built a million-dollar fortune in real estate says that the results are worth all the effort and problems!

So resolve *today* that you *will* consider using the MDM to build your real estate fortune. If you do take the big leap, I'm sure you'll be happy. And even if you don't take the leap, you'll still be happy because you've learned something. But I can also tell you this:

Not taking the leap will probably make you less happy than taking it!

### Points to Remember

- Income residential property can easily make you a millionaire.
- The biggest fortunes made by beginners in real estate are in older income buildings.
- There are seven easy, lucky steps to getting started in income property.
- You can build a fortune in both single- and multi-family income units.

- Zero-investment fortune building is easier in income property than in many others.
- OPM–Other People's Money–works for you in income property.
- Grow rich using the MDM–Million-Dollar-Method–in income property.

# 8

# CAPTURE RICHES IN COMMERCIAL AND INDUSTRIAL PROPERTY

Your first seven chapters showed you some of the riches you can build in residential real estate and raw land. Now you're ready to see how you can capture riches in commercial and industrial property.

### KNOW WHAT COMMERCIAL PROPERTY IS

Commercial property is real estate which is rented, leased, built, or sold for use in commercial or business activities. Thus, commercial property includes:

- Stores
- Factories
- Mobile home parks
- Garages
- Parking lots
- Shopping centers
- Office buildings
- Any other property for business use

Property rented out for factories and manufacturing plants of various types is often called *industrial real estate.* And property that is rented out for stores, theatres, etc., is usually called *commercial real estate.* But in this book we will use the term commercial for both types because it is easier to understand.

You can make a big fortune from commercial property—if you know how to acquire and rent this type of property. But you can also lose every penny you have (or borrow) if you carelessly select and rent commercial property. Let's see how you can make your real estate fortune in profitable rental property.

### LEARN THE UNIVERSAL RULE OF RENTALS

Most of the steady income in commercial property is earned from rentals. By steadily buying or building commercial or industrial rental units you can gradually increase your clear cash money-in-fist (MIF) rental income from zero to $25,000, or more, per month. Plenty of commercial real estate operators earn an income in this range. But those that do this well know the universal rule of rentals.

What *is* the universal rule of commercial real estate? It is:

> As an owner of commercial or industrial rental real estate, you are part of your tenant's business—should his business fail, your real estate investment could be in serious trouble.

Knowing this rule, you can keep out of money problems in commercial and industrial real estate. Here's how.

### HOW TO MAKE BIG MONEY IN REAL ESTATE

To make big money in commercial or industrial rental real estate use these seven magic tips:

1. Pick your tenants with care.
2. Check the credit rating of each prospective tenant.
3. Insist on a 3-month security deposit from each tenant.
4. Use a 2-year, or longer, lease for each tenant.
5. Don't pay for improvements of the rented quarters—have the tenant pay for all improvements.
6. Refuse to pay for special electric or other power needs of your tenants—this can break you faster than you think.

7. Try to arrange to receive a percentage of the profits of your tenants when you rent shopping-center and similar commercial property.

Knowing these methods, you are ready to start building your wealth. To start in commercial real estate, you might want to use my Real Estate Riches Method. It has worked well for others and I have high hopes that it will work for you.

### PROFITABLE REAL ESTATE RICHES METHODS

To hit it big in commercial real estate:

A. Find zero-cash property.
B. Take over the property.
C. Rent or lease all or part of the property to one or more suitable tenants.

These three steps sound simple. And they are simple—if you know what you're doing. Let's see how you can do things right from the first day you start to build your fortune in commercial real estate.

### FIND ZERO-CASH PROPERTY

There are a number of excellent real estate books available which I suggest you study after you finish this book. I've read many of these fine books and learned much from them. But the one drawback I found to all these books is that they assume you have money to start building your real estate empire!

My experience with Beginning Wealth Builders (BWBs) in many lands shows that most BWBs have very little money to start building their real estate empire. So that's why I concentrate on zero-cash real estate in this book. Further, you can use the methods I suggest whether you have money, or not!

You *can* find zero-cash real estate. It just:

• Takes you a little longer
• Requires more looking
• Needs more negotiating

While these needs may seem like hard work (and they are), I find that having to work harder:

• Gives you more fun in life
• Makes you more creative

- Improves your wealth-building skills
- Brings you riches sooner

So don't give up before you begin! At least listen to me to learn what kinds of money you can earn from zero-cash commercial real estate.

To find zero-cash commercial real estate:

1. Read the real estate ads in several large local newspapers every day, and on Sunday.
2. Read the monthly newsletter *International Wealth Success* *every* month of the year. It lists both zero-cash real estate and capital sources for property which you can buy using other people's money (OPM), giving you—in effect—zero-cash real estate.
3. List yourself with several real estate brokers who handle the type of property that interests you.
4. Send for the FREE government, city and state notices which list auctions of zero-cash and very low cash real estate. An IWS list of these sources is available FREE to subscribers to *International Wealth Success.*
5. Look for FOR SALE signs on property in your area. You can often work zero-cash deals with anxious owners who want to get out of their property responsibilities.
6. Watch for notices in your local newspaper of:

- Sheriff's auctions
- Bank disposals of property
- Tax lien sales
- Other low-priced sales

You can often buy such property using borrowed OPM giving you—in effect—zero cash property.

7. Get the word around to all your friends and business associates that you're in the market for zero-cash property. Advertise in your local paper, in IWS, and similar publications. You may soon have more offers than you can handle.

**Use Success-Directed Methods To Build Riches**

People talk to me in all sorts of places—such as in fancy restaurants, on planes and trains, at parties, etc.—about the big bundle of money they're going to make, when they get around to it. And they often have a "method" which they claim will build them a mountain of pure gold.

"Great!" I tell them. "Have you tried your method yet?" "No," comes the answer, "but someday soon I will."

I've tried my methods and they *do* work. And others have tried my zero-cash methods in many different fields—such as real estate, business, mail order, etc.—and proven that they *do* work for them, too. Like this letter from a reader: "Using many of Ty's ideas (I read all his books I can get my hands on), we have established a new alternative-life-style magazine. Eight months ago we took in something like $200 for the month. Last month we grossed over $5,000 (from our HOME) and this month we will do even better. _____ is now test-marking the magazine, we are selling a mail-order line of books and we can see $2,000,000 a year coming up . . . all from a home start using Ty's ideas."

### UPGRADE YOUR ZERO-CASH PROPERTY

Zero-cash commercial real estate will often need repairs, new tenants, and other improvements. Once you start to make such changes you can raise the rents you charge, thereby improving your income from the property. And since rent controls may not apply to commercial property, you don't have to worry about this aspect of government regulation.

To get the most profit from the improvements to your property which you make, or authorize:

1. Try to get your tenants to pay for the improvements. This helps you operate on larger amounts of OPM than just your mortgage.
2. Work with a contractor to have the tenants' work done. Collect a percentage fee on his work as your commission for giving the job to him. (Be sure the tenant knows of, and approves of, this fee—if your attorney so advises you).
3. Raise the rent of each tenant for whom you: (a) pay for improvements, (b) supervise or plan the improvements, or (c) work with the contractor on the improvements on a fee or any other basis.
4. Once you have rent increases in effect for one group of tenants, raise the rents for the remaining tenants in the building.

5. Ask for—and get—a percentage of the *gross* income earned by your tenants in the improved quarters, if you don't have such an arrangement now. If you do, then increase the percentage of the gross which you are to receive.
6. Build a reputation as a money-hungry landlord who treats tenants well but expects, and gets, top rents.

## GET IN ON THE BIG MONEY ACTION

The author whose book you're reading has grossed over a million dollars from his various business ventures. So I know what I'm talking about when I suggest that you get in on the big-money action. To do this you:

> Arrange to take a percentage of the business income of firms or people you serve—that is, get others to work for you while you invest nothing more than the time needed to sign a piece of paper—i.e. an agreement that the firms or people pay you part of their gross income.

The sharing in the gross income of a business which rents your building, land, or other real estate is a common practice. The typical percentage you can charge is two to five percent of the gross income your tenant earns in the premises he or she rents from you. Let's glance at an example of how this might work for you.

Your tenant rents a store from you in a shopping center you own. The tenant pays you $2,000 a month in rent. Your lease agreement with the tenant states that you will receive 3% of the gross sales in *this* store. So, besides the $2,000 a month rent, you'll receive one of the following amounts each month, depending on how much gross business the tenant does:

| Monthly Gross Business, $ | Your Share, $ |
| --- | --- |
| 1,000 | 30 |
| 5,000 | 150 |
| 10,000 | 300 |
| 25,000 | 750 |
| 50,000 | 1,500 |
| 100,000 | 3,000 |

| | |
|---|---|
| 150,000 | 4,500 |
| 200,000 | 6,000 |
| 250,000 | 7,500 |

The beauty of this setup for you and your fortune-building work is that:

> The harder your tenant works and the larger his gross income becomes, the higher the rent payments you receive.

And with your lease agreement based on the tenant's *gross* sales, your income is assured, whether the tenant makes a profit or not! So be sure to have your agreement written the way I recommend. Why? Because your success is tied in with that of your tenant!

But you have an ace card at all times, namely, your lease. Your tenant *has* to pay his rent to you. Thus, for this store, you are assured of getting at least $24,000 a year in rent, no matter how poor his business might be!

You *can* get a business-share clause in every commercial lease you write—if you offer tenants a good location and adequate facilities. Your commercial property will have these fortune-building features if you follow the profit-laden ideas you get throughout this book. Let's now take a close and careful look at each of the types of commercial properties listed at the start of this chapter.

## USE STORES TO BUILD A FAST FORTUNE

Stores can be large or small, grouped or single, one story or multi-story. Important aspects to keep in mind are:

- *Profit Potentials:* Get a percentage of the gross *plus* a profitable monthly rental for each store. Try to get store complexes—that is two or more stores per location (sometimes called shopping strips). Use long leases—5, 10, 20, or more years—where you have a tenant with a long history of profitable business. Limit new firms to short leases—1, 2, or 3 years, at the most. Make your tenants pay for all improvements; collect commissions on these whenever you can.

- *Risk Factors:* Never rent to new untried businesses if you can get experienced tenants. Be careful of single stores—you can go broke fast when a single store is vacant. Try to get yourself a shopping center sooner than later—if stores are your way of building great wealth fast. When you're low on cash, use the syndicate method (covered in another chapter) to raise money to buy, build, or improve a shopping center.

## TRY FACTORIES FOR A STEADY INCOME

Factories and industrial plants can give you steady rental income. And when you get tired of a steady income (as some people do) you can almost always arrange to sell your factory to the company that is renting it from you, or to another firm needing industrial space!

• *Profit Potentials:* Try to rent only to proven firms; demand the right to see and evaluate the financial statements for the three years prior to the year the firm applies for space in your premises. Get, whenever possible, a lease which gives you a percentage of the gross, plus a fixed monthly or annual rental. Sign a short lease (1 or 2 years) the first time with a new tenant; sign a longer lease *after* he proves his reliability.

• *Risk Factors:* Watch for signs of business troubles—such as slow payment of rent, checks that bounce, bad debts with other firms. Be tough and firm in all rent problems. Move in fast when you spot signs of money troubles. Charge your tenants for every improvement request. Have your tenants pay for the water, electricity, gas, oil, heat, and other utilities they use.

## GET IN ON THE AUTO BOOM

One of the differences between the capitalistic and socialistic countries of this world is the automobile. (We have millions; the socialists have only thousands). Though you may hate the auto (I love my Caddie), the car, truck, and motor bike can make you a fortune. How? By the rent their owners pay you for the garages you own.

Your garages can be of two main types: (1) active; (2) inactive. In an *active* garage you have a staff to:

- Pick up and deliver cars
- Wash and polish cars
- Do routine auto maintenance
- Store cars for extended periods
- Sell gas, oil, parts, and accessories

Thus, in an active garage you get income from two sources: (1) storage; (2) service.

In an *inactive* garage you obtain income from only one source—storage. You may have a small staff to park and fetch cars, but that's all. The inactive garage can be a real money machine when it's located downtown in a large city—New York, Chicago, Detroit, Dallas, Los Angeles, San Francisco, etc. But the downtown garages are more expensive to buy than suburban garages on the outskirts of a city.

Suburban garages tend to have a steady, predictable income because people keep their cars in them for years. Your downtown garage, in contrast, can have highly cyclical income. Thus, you'll make a bundle on theatre matinee days if you're in the theatre district. The same will be true for you on big shopping days.

One of the huge payoffs in garages can come 10, 20, or 30 years after you buy the garage. Land values can zoom in your area and the land your garage sits on can be worth many times what you paid for the garage. You sell out for a huge gain—after having had years of profitable income from your garage.

- *Profit Potentials:* Charge high prices for your garage space. Demand payment in advance for monthly and weekly rentals. Give *good* service to your customers. Know what your competition is charging and reduce your rates to below those of your competitors when you begin to lose tenants. Keep good income and expense records.

- *Risk Factors:* Set up fire safety standards for your garages so you don't have any claims which can skyrocket your insurance payments. Be careful to prohibit the storage of fuel, oily rags and other flammable materials in any containers other than those approved by fire underwriters and local fire regulations. When your garage personnel deliver and pick up cars as part of your service, be certain that your drivers are properly insured and bonded.

## BUILD A PATCH OF LAND INTO WEALTH

Parking lots are seldom more than a patch of land in a place where people want to park their cars. Add a little blacktop and a watchman's shack and you're in business. In some areas where land is really scarce—such as downtown Washington, D.C.—you may want to install simple, low-cost hydraulic lifts so you can park two cars in the space usually occupied by one. This allows you to double your income from the same patch of land.

To me, the parking lot is the simplest business known to man. Your only fixed expenses are:

- Land taxes
- Attendant's salary
- Electricity (in some cases)

And if you want to cut out the attendant's salary, you can install parking meters in your lot. Then you can have a part-time checker who looks into your lot once or twice a day. He can also empty the parking meters once every third day. Your part-timer's salary will be much lower than that of a full-time attendant.

- *Profit Potentials:* Parking-lot profits come from parking *activity*—the more cars you park, the higher your profits because your land doesn't cost you any more when it has 100 cars on it than when it has 1 car on it. Treat parked cars with care and you'll have plenty of repeat business. Use smart rates—high hourly charges for busy times, lower charges for slack periods and for overnight parking.

- *Risk Factors:* Since your parking lot is a *cash* business, take steps to control carefully the renting of space and the collection of money for the rental. Be certain that your attendants (if you use them) are safe drivers—damaged cars can waste your time and money. Try to buy parking-lot land which will have future "higher" use—such as for a building site. Then you can have the potential of a high capital gain on the sale of your land, after you've made good parking-lot profits for years.

## GET IN ON THE OFFICE BUILDING BOOM

Businesses everywhere—including your own business—need more and more office space. And you can get in on this booming demand for office space if you know how.

To build or buy your first office building using your own money is almost unheard of these days. Instead, you use OPM—other people's money. You can get OPM in various ways, such as:

- Borrowing from banks
- Forming a real estate syndicate
- Using a limited partnership
- Making a public stock offering
- Forming a REIT—Real Estate Investment Trust

You can get full information on each of these methods from IWS, Inc., Bank Plaza, Merrick, NY 11566, as follows:

| | |
|---|---|
| Borrowing: | *Business Capital Sources*, book, $15; also *2,500 Active Money Lenders for Real Estate*, book, $25. |
| Real estate syndicates: | *Real Estate Fortune Builders Program*, course, $99.50. |
| Limited partnerships: | *"Starting Millionaire" Program*, course, $99.50. |
| Public stock offering: | *Financial Broker-Finder-Business Broker-Consultant Program*, course, $99.50. |
| Forming a REIT: | *Real Estate Fortune Builders Program*, course, $99.50. |
| Unusual financing methods: | *Fast Financing Techniques for Real Estate Wealth*, course, $99.50. |

Using any of the above methods you can more easily get the money you need for a new or existing office building. And the beauty of an office building is that—with carefully selected tenants—you:

- Are paid your rents on time
- Have few tenant complaints
- Can sign long-term leases

- Are able to operate with absentee-management
- Get good tax deductions

Lenders—in general—like to make loans on well-built office buildings because:

- Their income is dependable
- There are few loan defaults
- The interest rate is fair to all

- *Profit Potentials:* Charge high rents for your office space. Keep your building in topnotch condition at all times. Have your tenants pay for all improvements they make in their space. Insist on liberal rent security payments. Invest these payments to your own advantage, using all the legal avenues open to you.

- *Risk Factors:* Avoid long leases (more than a year) with new firms. Never pay for improvements after a tenant has signed a lease, unless you agreed to make such improvements to induce the tenant to sign the lease.

## PYRAMID YOUR WAY TO COMMERCIAL-PROPERTY WEALTH

You *can* get richer quicker in commercial real estate. But to build your wealth faster, you have to use your head and your ingenuity. Here are a few lucky ways you can use, starting this very moment.

1. Locate OPM sources you can tap when you find the right deal. Use the books *Business Capital Sources* and *2,500 Active Money Lenders for Real Estate* mentioned earlier.
2. Look for, and advertise for, commercial property of the type you seek. You can advertise free of charge in the monthly newsletter *International Wealth Success,* if you are a 1-year, or longer, subscriber.
3. Choose the property you want to buy, after you look at several. Note that you may not need a large down payment for your commercial property—some of these properties are turned over for as little as a $1 down payment!
4. Borrow the money you need for the down payment. Use the IWS *"Starting Millionaire" Program* as a source of borrowing ideas.

5. Take over the property. On the usual office building you will earn a return of 8 to 9% on your investment—if you operate the building in the conventional, conservative way. But if you really swing in your management, as we've already discussed, you can earn as much as 20% on your investment. Since you're investing borrowed money, your return is really much higher. (Shopping centers typically earn 6%-8% on the investment).

One of the fastest ways to pyramid your way to commercial property wealth is by using the *Inflation Factor* in your property appraisals. Here's how:

### BUILD THE WORTH OF YOUR HOLDINGS

Let's say you take over a $200,000 office building for $20,000 down. You borrow the down payment by taking out a $25,000 36-month second-mortgage property loan. Three days after you apply for your loan you have $25,000 in the form of a $25,000 check. You use the extra $5,000 above the down payment for paying the closing costs on the building.

Now you call this first office building "Bldg. A." Two months after you buy Bldg. A you discover a second attractive and profitable office structure, Bldg. B. The price of this building is $215,000. You buy Bldg. B, but you get this second building easier, and faster. Here's how.

You go out in front of Bldg. A for which you "paid" $200,000 and study its appearance. "Gee," you say to yourself, "in the last two months the value of this building has risen, in *my* opinion, from $200,000 to $225,000—particularly when you consider the major impact of inflation on real estate values, and the improvements I've made and plan to make." So when you apply for the loan you need for the down payment you list the value of Bldg. A as:

| | |
|---|---|
| Estimated replacement price | = $225,000 |
| Owed = Price – down payment | = 180,000 |
| Your "equity" | = $ 45,000 |

So your net worth has risen by $45,000, based on your own appraisal of the building. With such a net worth it is easy for you to borrow the $25,000 down payment you need for Bldg. B.

Now let me make one very important point about building the worth of your holdings. This point is:

> It is perfectly legal for you to use *your* own estimated valuation of your property on your financial statement because this valuation is your opinion. And—in this world—a man or woman is still entitled to his or her opinion.

The Inflation Factor approach takes into consideration two items in your real estate life:

1. Inflation is constantly increasing the value of *your* real estate.
2. Inflation is constantly increasing the value of the improvements *you* make in your real estate.

And note that you can make all kinds of improvements in your real estate. Some of these improvements will cost you cold, hard cash. Other improvements will be what I call the "ghost" type—such as:

- Raising the rent of the tenants
- Reducing maintenance expenses
- Getting a better grade of tenants

These, and similar improvements, cost you little, or no, money. Yet by making these improvements you increase the income from your property. And whenever you raise the income of a piece of real estate, you automatically raise its value. The higher the value of a property, the greater *your* borrowing power on the property!

## CONTINUE BUILDING YOUR PROPERTY VALUES

Using the estimated—or appraised-value approach for your improved properties, you can quickly build your real estate holdings. Thus, Chris T. took over $1,200,000 worth of buildings in 11 months. Yet he started with zero cash! But he worked hard to improve the condition and income of each of his propertics so that his borrowing power rose every time he took over a building. A score sheet Chris prepared looked like this:

| Building | Month Acquired | Price | Borrowed Down Payment |
|----------|----------------|-------|-----------------------|
| A | 1 | $ 175,000 | $ 20,000 |
| B | 3 | 325,000 | 35,000 |
| C | 6 | 260,000 | 22,000 |
| D | 8 | 140,000 | 15,000 |
| E | 11 | 300,000 | 32,000 |
| | Total | $1,200,000 | $124,000 |

Of the $124,000 down payment, Chris didn't put up a dime! He borrowed the first $25,000 using a bank loan. From there on, Chris used each of the buildings as either part, or complete, collateral for the loans giving him the down payment on the next building.

This method of building wealth is called *pyramiding, leveraging,* or *zero-cash takeovers.* Why? Because you use:

- Borrowed money to start
- Appreciated (increased) values as collateral
- More borrowed money based on your appreciated collateral
- Continuation of the pyramid or lever using borrowed money (zero cash) and increased property values

### SEE THE REAL WORTH OF PROPERTY

Let's say that you're interested in shopping centers as a source of real estate income. You and a group of friends build a $20-million center, using borrowed money to pay for the land, construction, and all other expenses, including your, and your friends', salaries.

Do you know what your shopping center is worth the day you finish it—and before you have one tenant? Your $20-million center is now a product, just like a bar of soap, a refrigerator, a car, etc. Your $20-million shopping center is worth at least $30-million the day you finish it! And if you have a few top-rated tenants in the center, your shopping center will be worth close to $35-million the day it opens!

What all this means is important to you in your wealth-building activities, namely:

The act of buying and improving land (putting up buildings, etc.) earns you a profit anywhere in the world.

In any real estate construction deal you can earn money two ways:

1. Your salary, which is paid out of borrowed construction funds, while the project is being put up
2. Your profit if you want to sell the project as soon as it is finished

Now let's say you *don't* want to sell your $20-million shopping center which you finished yesterday. Instead, you want to hold onto it and collect nice fat rent checks every month. So what do you do? You go out and get 100%, or better, long-term—20, 30, or 40 years—financing. Let's see how this works.

## BORROW YOUR WAY TO REAL ESTATE WEALTH

To build a commercial property such as a shopping center, you:

1. Locate the land you need
2. Borrow the money for the land down payment
3. Have preliminary construction plans prepared
4. Borrow construction funds for putting up the center
5. Build the center
6. Borrow the long-term money for the mortgage on the center

## GET 100% FINANCING FOR YOUR DEALS

Your shopping center (or any other commercial development) cost you—we'll say—$20-million to put up. You have it appraised on completion and the value put on it is $30-million.

Depending on money conditions at the time you apply for your long-term mortgage, you can get 80% of the appraised value, or $24-million, in a tight-money market, or 90%, or $27-million in a loose—or easy-money market.

Figuring 10% for closing fees, points, and other costs, you walk away with either $2-million or $5-million for your "trouble" in building the shopping center. Since you'll probably have other people in on the deal with you, your personal take will be somewhat lower.

And by keeping title to the shopping center you will probably be able to net about 9% on your income from the center. This should give you a cash income of at least $100,000 a year. And for the first ten years or so, your cash income will probably be completely—or nearly completely—tax free because of the depreciation tax shelter you get on the buildings. So you see, it *is* possible to get full 100% financing of your commercial real estate deals.

In this deal, if you received a $24-million long-term mortgage, you'd be operating with 120% financing. With a $27-million long-term mortgage, you'd have 135% financing. And note this:

> Any money you get above what you need for long-term financing may be completely tax free to you because it is a loan, and the proceeds of a loan are usually tax-free.

For a full discussion of a variety of 100% financing methods, be sure to see my book *How to Borrow Your Way to a Real Estate Fortune,* available from IWS, Inc., for $15, at the address mentioned earlier.

### WHY REAL ESTATE RISES IN VALUE

If you're wondering why a shopping center costing you $20-million to build is worth $30-million, or more, on completion, just glance at the following facts:

*Building material costs* increase an
  average of 1% per month
*Land costs* increase an average of
  15% a year
*Labor costs* increase an average of
  10% a year

So while you're building your shopping center its value is rising because the prices of the items you bought for the center (materials, land, labor) are rising! This is true of all real estate.

### CAPTURE COMMERCIAL-PROPERTY RICHES

There are billions to be made from commercial and rental property deals of all kinds. Here are a few examples of how other people—just like yourself—made *BIG* money in commercial property, starting with little or no cash and operating on borrowed money.

### Fourplexes Build Wealth

Mary T. borrowed $200 from her uncle to take over a 4-store mini-mall (which had been taken over by the city for non-payment of taxes) in a depressed neighborhood for no cash down. Within three months she owned *every* fourplex store on both sides of the street—a total of ten. Yet she didn't have to put a cent of her own down for one building. Sticking to fourplexes because she likes their easy renting and care, Mary T. now has a total of 80, giving her 320 store rental units. At an average monthly rental of $100, Mary T's income is $32,000 per month, or $384,000 a year, before expenses. Since her expenses are low, Mary is making a fast bundle without having put up a penny!

### Garages Are Money Makers

Tim K. is an auto mechanic who tired of working for hourly wages while his boss grew rich from Tim's labors. So Tim decided to become a boss himself. But on looking at the risks and rewards in running a gas station and repair shop, Tim decided he wanted something different. "What I wanted—and still want—is a steady, stable, predictable income," Tim says.

Checking around, Tim decided that auto garages would give him the kind of income he sought, and needed. But Tim's problem was—like that of so many other Beginning Wealth Builders (BWBs)—how to get the money to buy his first garage. When Tim called me about his money problems, I told him that he should go at raising the money he needed in two ways:

1. Seek out lenders everywhere
2. Try to get one or two zero-cash garages

Now why did I recommend these *two* approaches? Because they would give Tim maximum leverage in finding, and taking over, the garages he needed. Tim also studied current issues of *Business Capital Sources*, and *International Wealth Success*, both of which give the names of hundreds of lenders. And, as a trial, Tim applied for a $10,000 loan from several lenders. *All* approved his application in a day!

But the day Tim's loan applications were approved, a better event occurred. Tim was offered a zero-cash garage. Here's how this happened.

Tim had spread the word that he was looking for a zero-cash garage. When the owner of an old, but money-making, garage passed away, the family immediately contacted Tim. The family knew Tim to be honest and dependable. Knowing that he didn't have much money, the family offered Tim the garage:

- For *no cash down*
- With a 20-year pay-off time
- In an *as-is* condition

Tim jumped at the chance. In three months he had the garage looking like new and fully rented to its 200-car capacity.

Next Tim invited several local bankers in to see his garage. While showing them through the garage, Tim told the bankers of his interest in buying a string of good garages. "That's a great idea," said one of the bankers. "If you need any help, just give us a ring. We'll be glad to study your deal."

Tim did call this banker when he found the next profitable garage. The banker liked the deal and Tim got a loan for $50,000 for the down payment on the garage. Today Tim has ten well-maintained garages which give him an income of more than $100,000 a year. "Not bad for an ex-auto mechanic," Tim says proudly as he shows you around his neat garages.

### GO WHERE THE MONEY IS

There's big, big money in commercial real estate. And you can easily make some of this big money yours! All it takes is:

- A desire to *be* rich
- Drive to find what *you* want
- Careful deals with an eye on profits
- Constant expansion until you reach your income goal

To prove to yourself that you *can* hit commercial real estate big money, just put some of my hints into action. I guarantee you that you won't be sorry you did! Get started today—*now*.

### Points to Remember

- As an owner of commercial property you are part of your tenant's business.
- Pick your commercial tenants with extreme care.
- Insist on rent security deposits from commercial tenants.

- Try to get a share of the gross income from every commercial tenant you have.
- Look for—and find—zero-cash commercial property.
- Use the increased value of your property as collateral for additional loans to buy more commercial real estate.

# 9

## HOW TO WHEEL AND DEAL WITH LEVERAGE IN PROPERTIES

A wheeler-dealer is a person who buys, sells, or deals in real estate properties of all kinds. As a wheeler-dealer your main goal is to make money quickly by buying low and selling high. And one nice feature of being a wheeler dealer is that you *don't* need any type of:

- License
- Permit
- Registration
- Certificate
- Diploma
- College (or even high-school) education

Let's see how we can make *you* a highly successful real estate wheeler-dealer in a short time.

### WHAT YOU'LL DO AS A WHEELER-DEALER

A wheeler-dealer will do anything *honest* to make money. But in the real estate field, you may, as a wheeler-dealer:

- Buy cheap; sell high
- Operate on 100% to 150% financing
- Never really *own* anything
- Run your office from your head
- Spend more time *not* working than working
- Get rich in a hurry

Let's put you into the easiest money you've ever earned by making you a wheeler-dealer in real estate properties of various kinds.

## BUY CHEAP; SELL HIGH

Let's say that you work a deal just like one young wheeler-dealer, Lennie S., worked recently. Here's what he did, and what *you* might also do.

Step 1: Buy 75 acres of raw land for $1 down per acre. (Total cost of the land is $7,500).

Step 2: Go to your local zoning board and have the land use category changed from industrial to commercial-residential.

Step 3: Contact a builder and suggest that he consider putting up a combined office-apartment house tower on the land.

Step 4: Send news releases to your local papers telling them about the plans and suggestions.

Step 5: "Talk up" your idea and project wherever you go in your local area.

If you obtain the same results as Lennie did, you'll sell 50 acres of the land to the builder for $4,000 per acre, for a profit of $192,500. You find your gross profit by subtracting your land cost, $7,500 here, from your land selling price, or $200,000 here. And since you sold only 50 of the 75 acres, you still have 25 acres left. Hopefully, you can also sell these acres at a big profit some time in the future.

## KNOW THE BASICS OF WHEELING AND DEALING

As a wheeler-dealer you will use—again and again—several basic concepts. These are:

- Profitable ideas
- Unique approaches
- Carefully planned publicity
- Belief in your ideas
- Patience to wait for the big deal
- Charging high prices for your ideas

In the deal described above, you used a profitable idea (buying the raw land), a unique approach (having the zoning changed), carefully planned publicity (news releases to newspapers, personal contacts), and belief in your ideas, to net yourself a big bundle of profit.

You will, of course, use other approaches and methods when you're wheeling and dealing. But you'll develop these as you gain experience with people in various businesses around the country. For you'll find that while your basic activity is real estate, your deals will vary when you work with people and firms having different uses for the land or building you are handling.

## BE WELCOME WHEREVER YOU GO

You—let's say—are working at a fairly interesting and moderately well paying job. But you want to wheel and deal—particularly in real estate. Suddenly you're given a four-week "vacation" (without pay) from your job. "I really don't know what to do with the time," you say to me during a telephone conversation about your future. "I'd sure like to turn it into some extra income."

"Why don't you come with me on my next business trip for two weeks and I'll show you how to make some extra money as a wheeler-dealer," I reply.

You agree to come along. "I'll show you how to be welcome *wherever* you go," I promise with a laugh. "You'll learn the one specialty which all wheeler-dealers push."

"That's exactly what I've always wanted to know," you say happily.

Wheeler-dealers throughout the world have one specialty which they *all* plug when they're looking for new business. That specialty is: *Finding the money a business or individual needs to complete a specific deal.*

Yes, that's right, as a successful wheeler-dealer you'll be welcome everywhere in this world if you can:

- Find money for your clients
- Arrange financing for a deal
- Negotiate a loan
- Place a mortgage with a lender
- Pick lenders for a deal
- Process loan applications for a client

Now don't let this list frighten you. You're about to learn how you can have 99% of this work done for you by others at a very low cost and hardly any investment of *your* time or money. Knowing how to have others do most of your work for you will make you a big success because:

> The wheeler-dealer who can bring money to a deal is welcome everywhere in this world because every business needs money at some time during its history.

My own personal observation—with which you may, or may not agree—is that:

> Every small business I've ever been close to can always use some extra cash!

So if you can come up with the needed cash in the form of a loan which you obtain, you'll be doubly welcome by almost *every* business, everywhere! And let me tell you this, good friend, it's a lot easier to do business when you're welcome than when you have to spend a lot of your time and energy selling people your ideas!

## KNOW WHERE THE MONEY IS

As a real estate wheeler dealer you'll run across deals where you'll want to find money for:

- Property down payments
- Mortgages—1st, 2nd, 3rd, etc.
- Building and property improvements
- Construction of buildings of all kinds
- Standby purposes
- Takeouts
- Wraparounds
- Other

Knowing how, and where, to get this money can get you in on
deals you might otherwise lose.

And how can you get the knowledge you need to set up loan
deals for the clients you get? The best way that I know of is to
study and use the IWS *Financial Broker-Finder-Business Broker-
Consultant Program.* This hard-hitting *Program* contains some
eight easy-to use Speed-Read books which show you *exactly* how
to:

- Set up your own financial-broker business
- Arrange financing deals
- Get the money you need
- Find lenders (thousands of names and addresses are given
  you in the Program)
- Take a company public to get money that does *not* have to
  be repaid

With this easy-to-understand *Program Course* on hand you should
be able to start wheeling and dealing within a few days after you
receive it. Costing only $99.50, this big *Program* can be ordered
from IWS Inc., Bank Plaza, Merrick, NY 11566. Send a money
order or certified check for fast, special-delivery service. The big
money book, *Business Capital Sources for Financial Brokers,*
which lists more than a thousand money sources, is included in the
*Program.*

### OPERATE ON 100% FINANCING

Plenty of real estate wheeler dealers never put up a cent of their
own money. Instead, they operate entirely on borrowed money,
or 100% financing.

To run your business on OPM—other people's money—you have
to:

- Line up some lenders
- Find one or more good deals
- Take action on a deal
- Bring the money and deal together

Let's see how you might use 100% OPM to put a few deals
together.

## MAKE OPM WORK FOR YOU

In almost every real estate deal you'll ever swing the biggest part of it is defined by a five letter word: *Money*. Sure, you may have a few temporary problems with items like the title search, escrow account, utilities approval, etc. But these problems are minor—if you have the money needed for the deal.

For instance, let's say that you, like another Beginning Wealth Builder (BWB) named Ken T., spot an ad for a factory building for sale in your area. You check out the building and find that it is:

- Available for $25,000 cash down
- Has three good tenants; one unreliable tenant
- Of sturdy construction
- Might be sold at a profit, or could be held and run at a profit

You have your lenders lined up and ready to advance you the money you need. (You lined up your lenders in advance by using the methods in the IWS *Financial Broker Program*. Briefly, you called on local prospective lenders, told them of your plans to wheel and deal in real estate and asked them if they'd be willing to lend you money on the *right* deal. Several said yes; a few said no).

Wheeling and dealing, you offer $18,000 down for the factory. In making this offer you are using Hicks' First Rule of Wheeling and Dealing, namely:

**Rule 1**

> Never offer to pay any asking price for anything. Always try to negotiate a reduced price.

For instance, say that the seller finds your $18,000 offer on the above factory unacceptable. The most he can do is say: "No; I won't sell at that price." If you still want the factory (or any other property for that matter), you can raise your offer.

You do raise your offer for this property—to $20,000. This is still not attractive to the seller. So you go to $22,000. He accepts. You've thus saved yourself $3,000, or more than 10% of the asking down payment.

Contacting your lender friends, you describe the deal to them They ask for more information in an organized arrangement and give you some forms to fill out. The forms are really a comprehensive loan application which you fill out and have typed up. Three days later *two* lenders call. Both say: "Your application has been approved! Come on over and pick up your money." You decide which lender you'd like to work with, and get your check.

### PUT ACTION INTO YOUR PLANS

Three weeks after your loan application is approved you take over the factory. As you analyzed it earlier, you may be able to either sell the factory quickly, or rent it at a good profit.

To find buyers you publicize the future availability of the factory—starting the day your loan is approved. You get free publicity through your friends, local business and trade associations, the IWS Newsletter, and similar outlets. While you do not receive any firm offers before you take over the factory, you get several interesting "nibbles." One of these, you hope, will pay off in the future. Thus, you've *actionized* your plans.

### FOLLOW THROUGH ON YOUR PLANS

You continue to try to sell the factory. Meanwhile you take other actions, namely you:

- Improve parts of the building
- Raise rents for all tenants
- Try to find the unreliable tenant another factory he can rent

So far your wheeling and dealing has been typical of what any other ambitious beginner might do. But suddenly you have an unusual chance. Let's see how you react. Here's what happens.

Your unreliable tenant—a small electronics company—stops paying its rent. You wait two months to see what will happen. Nothing does happen, so far as being paid the rent owed to you. But the owner of the electronics company does tell you that he'd like to sell out his business—cheap. Your ears perk up as soon as you hear the word *cheap* because that's how most wheeler-dealers try to get the items they take over.

You think—for a few hours—about the possibility of taking over the electronics company. While you know almost *nothing* about electronics, you decide that now—today—is the time to start learning the facts of life about electronics. Why? Because you're a wheeler-dealer and you have a feeling that you're on to something that could make you rich!

So you call the owner of the electronics company and tell him: "I'll take the company off your hands for no cash down. Besides the company, I'll take all your debts, including the back rent. This means that you can walk away tomorrow—free and clear!"

"Sounds good," the owner replies. "But I need some 'mad' money until I find a job or start another company."

"How much do you need?" you ask. "Three- to five-thousand dollars," he replies. "I'll give you twenty-five hundred, and that's it," you say, again using Rule 1. "You have a deal," he says happily.

You hang up and wonder to yourself: "Did I do the right thing?" "Yes," you say to yourself, "I did." So you contact your lender friend immediately and tell him about your new deal. "Twenty-five hundred isn't any problem. In fact, you can pick it up right after lunch," he tells you.

## KEEP WHEELING AND DEALING

You visit your lender and get your money and go home to think things over. "I really want to wheel and deal in real estate," you say to yourself. "Electronics isn't my bag." But you're using the second Hicks Rule of wheeling and dealing, namely:

**Rule 2**

> Never turn down a good chance outside your main field of interest—if you can make money.

Sure, you want to specialize in real estate. But if you can make money in another field, go right to it.

So you take over the electronics company, using Rule 2, and borrowed money. But no sooner do you take over the firm than you learn that the main product is *not* a piece of electronic equipment, or a part. Instead, the main product is books on electronics! And these books are sold mainly overseas—not in the United States.

You take a deep breath and sigh—"Life isn't always as simple as you think it is." But wait, all is *not* lost. You *can* make money with *any* product—if you keep wheeling and dealing.

## EXPLORE NEW MARKETS

The wheeler-dealer never gives up. If he or she fails today he or she shrugs his or her shoulders, gets a good night's sleep, and starts trying all over again tomorrow. And since you're a confirmed wheeler-dealer, even though you're just starting, you decide to find out *why* this electronics firm you bought was going broke.

Two days' work shows you that the former owner:

* Made poor choices of ad outlets
* Delivered his products late
* Didn't send out bills on time
* Never built up a mailing list
* Knew little about product warehousing

Being an ambitious wheeler-dealer, you decide to correct these conditions. But to do so, you have to learn something about export-import! And to think that you started out to be a real estate tycoon! You grit your teeth and resolve to learn export-import. In making this resolution you are using the third Hicks Rule of wheeling and dealing, namely:

**Rule 3**

> Never let a lack of know-how stand in your way of making money. Get the know-how you need as fast as you can!

## FEED YOUR BRAIN TO FILL YOUR POCKETS

Your decision to be a go-go wheeler-dealer gives you the zip and drive to find good deals and make money from them. This same zip and drive can help you build your knowhow to solve practical business problems anywhere.

To learn export-import you buy a set of the IWS *"Starting Millionaire" Program* for $99.50 and a copy of their big book *How to Prepare and Process Export-Import Documents: A Completely Illustrated Guide,* $25.

With the *Program* and book in your home, you quickly learn how to handle the export of your new products. What's more, you also learn how to:

- Have an overseas business address without paying one cent in rent
- Sell overseas without having to register your company with any local government
- Store your products in a bonded warehouse overseas at *no* cost to you
- Get overseas loans for your customers so they pay *you* sooner
- Run ads in overseas publications
- Make mailings from an overseas point at a cost less than you'd pay at home
- Have money that is mailed to your overseas address sent to you at home for deposit in *your* bank
- Make money on foreign exchange
- Take many other profit-laden business steps at no expense other than the investment of a little time

While I'd like to tell you—here and now—how to take all these wheeler-dealer steps, we don't have enough space. Besides—this is a book on real estate, not export-import. Also, you can get all the facts you need from the IWS *"Starting Millionaire" Program* by sending $99.50 to IWS Inc., Bank Plaza, Merrick, NY 11566.

## BUILD SALES TO SELL AT A PROFIT

There are really only two kinds of wheeler-dealers in this world today—those who:

1. Take over a going business, improve the income, and then sell the business
2. Start a new business, build it to a profitable level, and then sell the business

You can make *big, big* money either way. But to do so you must keep the Hicks Rule 4 in mind at all times, namely:

**Rule 4**

Know why you're wheeling and dealing in every business deal. Then there's little chance of making a serious mistake.

When you're acting as a wheeler-dealer who's looking to sell a going business you took over, you know that, for best results, you must:

- Have the business showing good profits
- Appeal to the prospective buyer's desire for instant income
- Show a potential for some future growth

To achieve these goals for your newly acquired business you—as a beginning wheeler-dealer—take several sensible steps. Thus, you:

- Advertise your products
- Get the account books in order (plenty aren't)
- See that all taxes have been paid
- Actively look for new business
- Build up a good work force
- Run the business profitably
- Advertise the business for sale

### SELL OUT WHEN YOU'RE READY

You take these steps with your inherited business. Within a few days you're flooded with calls wanting to know more about the business you have for sale. During one of your discussions a prospect asks: "Do I have to keep the business in that factory?"

Like a flash you realize that you have a profitable deal in your hands. "Yes," you say, "for at least two years." The reason you answer this way is because you've decided that any person or firm that you allow to buy your business *must* have a good credit rating, because you'll insist on this being so. This means that they'll be reliable tenants. Also, you can keep an eye on the business. You are using the fifth Hicks rule of wheeling and dealing, namely:

**Rule 5**

> When you sell a business, arrange the deal so you have maximum control over the buyer for as long as possible—or until you get full payment.

Two weeks after you advertise the business for sale (and three months after you "bought" it for zero cash), you sell the business for $325,000. Of this total price you receive $50,000 in cash and promissory notes for $275,000, payable over three years. Thus, in just a few months you have:

- Bought and sold a business
- Received $50,000 in cash with zero investment of your own money
- Been given notes that will pay you nearly $100,000 a year for three years
- Found a new, and reliable tenant
- Have the chance to get your business back if the buyer can't pay off the notes
- Can sell the notes at a discount for fast cash

And two weeks after you sell the business you receive a $500,000 offer for the factory and the land it sits on. You agree to sell at this price, if the buyer will put $100,000 cash down. But he tries to wheel and deal with you, using his version of Rule 1. You combat the buyer with the Hicks Rule Six, namely:

**Rule 6**

> Never sell real estate, or any other valuable item, for a cash price less than what you seek. As a seller you have what a buyer wants; make him pay your price.

You stick to your guns and eventually the buyer comes up with $100,000 cash. Being a man of your word, you sell to him at the price of $500,000, with $100,000 cash down. You now have the following from the two businesses you've sold, less your cost:

*Cash:*   $150,000 - $22,000 = $128,000
*Notes:*  $675,000 in money owed to you that will be paid
off over a period of years.

Yet you did all this on OPM—other people's money! Sound impossible? It isn't! The deals worked here are made every day of the week somewhere in this great world of ours. And you *can do* the same—if you use the rules and hints you've learned thus far in this chapter.

### 12 SHORT HINTS FOR WHEELER-DEALERS

1. Make speed your goal in all deals.
2. Remember that a fast deal can be just as profitable (and often more profitable) than a slow, dragged-out deal.
3. Get good legal and accounting help.
4. Study carefully the tax laws for your business.
5. Find out if, and how, you can shelter any of your income from high taxes.
6. Get yourself some useful and profitable specialized know-how—such as being a *Financial Broker, Finder, Business Broker, Consultant*—as given by the IWS Program mentioned elsewhere in this book.
7. Use the six rules given in this chapter as guides to faster, easier, and higher profits as a wheeler-dealer.
8. Promote yourself and your business, using free ads whenever you can.
9. Be tough and aggressive in your business—your profits will soar if you demand, and get, your own way.
10. Try to create a *new* profit idea every day of the week. In wheeling and dealing, good ideas often pay your biggest profits.
11. Keep records of your deals. Try to use one notebook instead of many scraps of paper. One book will help you find your ideas at a later date and will clear up your thinking.
12. Push ahead continously—regardless of how rough things may seem. Though your luck may appear to have run out, it will often improve if you just push ahead one more foot, one more hour, one more day!

## THE BEST INVESTMENT ON EARTH

Man has gone to the moon—and will eventually go to other planets. Yet, as a sage once said: "The best investment on earth *is* earth." Since I firmly believe this to be so—and have put my money where my pen is (in my own real estate ventures)—I want to convince *you* of this fact.

If you wheel and deal according to the rules in this chapter you will not go wrong. Why? Because if you're careful in your buying of real estate the:

- Basic value of the property will remain
- Property values will seldom go down much
- Constant inflation pushes land values up
- Reduced amounts of land push prices up

So get yourself a piece of earth, using wheeling-and-dealing tactics. You may profit way beyond your wildest dreams in fields you never thought you'd enter.

### Points to Remember

- You can wheel and deal in real estate properties.
- No formal education, license, or other training is needed by wheelers and dealers.
- To make big money wheeling and dealing, look for profitable ideas and unique approaches.
- You can often operate on 100% financing when you wheel and deal.
- Make action, speed and new ideas the key forces in your wheeling and dealing work.

# 10

## USE UNUSUAL REAL ESTATE
## WEALTH TECHNIQUES

Just as there are millions of ways to make a million in business, so too are there millions of ways to make a million in real estate. In this chapter I'd like to give you a number of *unusual* ways to amass great wealth in your real estate deals. I hope that at least one of these ways makes you the bundle of money you seek.

### ISOLATE THE UNUSUAL

Every area, every type of land, every place under the sun has an unusual way that you can make money from it. Here are unusual ways you might consider using in your area. Each way has made money for a Beginning Wealth Builder (BWB) somewhere.

**Unusual Real Estate Wealth Techniques**

1. Specialize in islands
2. Handle only view-type properties
3. Concentrate on distressed-property sales
4. Fix up rundown properties for profits
5. Run motels with absentee management
6. Rent post offices to the Postal Service

Let's take a look at each of these techniques and see how *you* might use it to build a fast, easy-money fortune in your real estate deals. Or, if you don't like the method we give you, let's see how *you* can change it to suit *your* local conditions.

### SPECIALIZE IN ISLANDS

"No man is an island," yet every man and woman has a dreamy, soft spot in his heart for an island "away from it all." To check this out, watch the expression on a person's face when you casually mention: "I'm thinking of buying an island."

The *second home,* or vacation home, is *big* business around the world today. And a second home (or even a first home) on an island is always a salable item. By specializing in islands—with or without homes on them—you can build yourself a big real estate fortune quickly and easily.

Where can you find islands? The best ones are those off mainland coasts—such as:

- Maine
- Oregon
- North Carolina
- Florida
- California
- Texas
- New York
- Connecticut
- Canada
- Mexico
- South American countries
- European countries
- African countries

As a general guide you can say that:

The closer an island is to the mainland, the higher—in general—its value to you and others.

For this reason I recommend that—at the start—you specialize in islands no more than 5 miles (8.05 kilometers) off the mainland. And you'll find that islands within one mile off the mainland are usually the most popular.

Why are close-in islands more sought after than those further out? Because on an island your travel time to and from the mainland becomes a factor—particularly in bad weather. Since you almost always need a boat to get to and from an island (unless you can fly in and out, or use a bridge), the further the distance from the mainland, the longer the boat trip.

## HOW TO MAKE MONEY FROM ISLANDS

To make money from islands, take these steps:

1. Decide where you will concentrate your buying and selling by studying the areas you like.
2. Pick the size of the islands you'll work on—the smaller the better at the start.
3. Begin looking for suitable islands by scanning the ads in local newspapers, talking to people in the area you selected, and exploring by boat.
4. Once you find a few suitable islands, make offers to the owners. Use, as a guide, the tips on wheeling and dealing given in Chapter 9.
5. Sometimes your best approach is to put down only a *binder* to hold the island for 90, 120, or 180 days. The binder will cost you a lot less and—since you'll lose your binder if you don't buy the island or sell it to someone else—will act as a strong motivating force to make you find a buyer.

## PROMOTE YOUR ISLANDS IN UNUSUAL PLACES

Once you've picked a few islands to sell, you'll want to move them fast. You can get the action you seek if you promote and advertise in unusual places, such as:

- Boating magazines
- Camping publications
- Outdoors clubs
- Rifle associations
- Hunting clubs
- Bird watcher's clubs

Now note these facts about making money from island property:

1. You can't make money on islands in the middle of an ocean because people don't want to get *that* far away from it all.
2. Island buyers are usually also boaters, hunters, or out-doors people of some kind. Promote your islands to them and you'll move your "products" (land surrounded by water) faster.

## HOW ISLANDS CAN MAKE YOU MONEY

Here are a few typical examples of how Beginning Wealth Builders (BWBs) just like yourself have made BIG money wheeling and dealing in islands.

### Maine "Island" For Farmers

Chris T. heard of a Maine "island" for sale cheap—just $2,000. Having an area of 3 acres, this "island" was really only an island at high tide! At low tide you could walk from the island to the mainland, using a rocky reef connecting the two.

Chris put a binder of $100 down on the island with the understanding that he could hold it for 120 days. With the binder (which he borrowed from a local bank) paid, Chris set out to find a buyer for his island. But instead of searching for a real island buff, Chris reasoned this way:

There are plenty of men who'd love to own an island. But many of these men are married to gals who either don't like, or are afraid of, islands. So his job was to find such a couple.

Chris found the couple he wanted with a simple ad carrying the headline: "When Is An Island *Not* An Island?" The ad went on to describe how an island-seeking couple could have a 3-acre island at high tide and a 3-acre country estate at low tide. Chris ran his ad in a bird watcher's magazine. One month later he sold the island for $10,500—a neat profit on a $100 investment!

### Sell The Beach Not The Island

Elmer Wheeler is famous for his remark "Sell the sizzle—not the steak." Ken P. knew of Elmer when a beautiful 10-acre island came on the market in his area of Connecticut. Ken studied the island and decided—since the island had no buildings on it—that he'd have to sell something else—the sizzle.

Though the island had no houses, it did have a beautiful half-moon shaped sandy beach. It was this beach which became Ken's sizzle. But who would want an island without a house? Ken prepared a list of possible buyers:

- Yacht club
- Rifle club
- Bird watcher's groups
- Swimming clubs

Using his list as a guide, Ken contacted local clubs and associations *after* he took possession of the island for $500 down. In less than two weeks Ken had four bids for the island and within a month he sold out at a $5,000 profit.

### WHY ISLANDS ARE PROFITABLE

You *can* make money from islands because this type of property:

- Is often in rural areas
- Is generally for sale by novices
- Seldom is sold creatively
- Is not sought by too many people
- Can be difficult to sell fast

But you—with the knowhow I've given you here—can move island property fast. Just be sure the island isn't in the middle of an ocean. The middle of a small lake is fine from an investment standpoint but the middle of an ocean is bad!

Also remember that you can't act as a real estate broker in most states unless you are licensed. So check out your state to be sure. You can, of course, sell your personal real estate *without* a license—which is what was done in the above two deals.

### HANDLE ONLY VIEW-TYPE PROPERTIES

"I've always wanted a house with a view," said the pretty housewife. "I'd rather live in an apartment for ten years than to have a viewless cramped house in some little development."

This housewife was expressing the thoughts held by the house-with-view set. These people scrimp and save for years so they can buy their dream house—one with a view. And you can earn money by catering to their dreams. You can:

- Offer them land with a view
- Or offer them homes with a view

## KNOW THE VIEWS TO SELL

Basically there are only three kinds of views to sell:

1. Land views
2. Water views
3. A combination of (1) and (2)

Each of these kinds of views can be subdivided. Thus:

**Types of Land Views**

a. Mountains
b. Valleys
c. Plains
d. Populated areas

**Types of Water Views**

a. Ocean
b. Bay
c. River
d. Lake
e. Swamp or bayou

You can, of course, combine these types of views. For instance, some homes in California have an ocean view from the front and a mountain view from the back. Local zoning laws often recognize the importance of the view to the owner of property and prevent the partial or complete blocking of the view by construction of any type of permanent structure on adjacent land once the land is occupied.

To judge the view-value of a property, site, home, or apartment house, visit the area and then the actual property. Try to see the views as the owner of the property would when:

- Standing up
- Sitting down
- Relaxing in an easy chair
- In a garden
- Lounging by a swimming pool
- From any other position

Once you see the view from these and other positions, compare the view with that from other, competitive properties in the area. Then assign a dollar value to "your" view, based on the prices being charged for other view properties nearby.

When pricing a view property, keep this important fact in mind:

> The view from a property remains for years. Buildings can rise and fall but the view remains. So price the property more for its view than for its structures. (*Location gives the view and location remains forever*).

### PUSH VIEWS TO THE RIGHT PROSPECTS

Both boaters and non-boaters love water views. Boaters love to watch the boats and the water. Non-boaters love to watch boats and water, too. But they're far enough away so the non-boaters don't have to go near them!

Hunters, trappers, camping buffs, hikers, and similar enthusiasts like mountain views. And many "just plain folk" also like mountains, valleys, and plains. So your prospects are all over when it comes to land views.

To sell view property, push the one feature all prospects for this type of property seek—namely the *View*. Get to be known as the guy or gal who has the inside track on choice view property.

Kurt L. did exactly this in building a big fortune in view properties. Working on the west coast, Kurt specialized in businesses having a view. Thus, Kurt's first deal was a tavern overlooking the Pacific Ocean in LaJolla, California, just north of San Diego.

Kurt took over the tavern using $2,000 of borrowed money he obtained by taking a business loan from his bank. The total price of the tavern and the land was $12,000.

When Kurt took over the tavern its business was sluggish because the owner was more interested in sampling his own wares than in serving customers. Also, the owner had allowed the building to go to seed—windows were broken, the roof leaked, painting was needed inside and outside. Lastly the tavern lacked "character"—it had no focus for its patrons.

## GIVE THE PUBLIC WHAT IT WANTS

Kurt changed the tavern dramatically. "I want to give the public what it wants—a comfortable tavern with a view which has real character." Kurt borrowed $5,000 more from his bank and:

- Installed curved nooks overlooking the ocean
- Changed the bar so people looked out over the water
- Decorated the interior with South Sea island decor

Within weeks the tavern's income jumped from $1,000 a week to $6,000 a week. With business booming, Kurt put his view property up for sale. In a few days Kurt sold out for $80,000, for a total profit of $63,000, plus the money he'd taken in as a profit on the business while he was having the building interior and exterior improved.

Kurt didn't stop when he sold this tavern. Instead, he kept working his way north—buying, improving, and selling—always at a good profit, and always dealing in either ocean or mountain view taverns. Using this approach, Kurt has built a sizeable fortune quickly. And what's more, he's had great fun along the way!

Of course, there are many other types of view property from which you can make a profit. Taverns aren't the only kind of view property from which a man or woman can earn a fortune. You can also earn big *money from:*

- Apartment houses
- Shopping centers
- Industrial plants
- Mobile home parks
- Recreation parks
- Camping grounds

So don't give up! Keep looking until you find the right view property for your fortune building.

## CONCENTRATE ON DISTRESSED-PROPERTY SALES

This land of ours is full of distressed properties—that is structures and land that was:

- Abandoned by the owners
- Taken over for non-payment of taxes

• Discarded because of building-code violations
• Left because of fear of new tenants

Distressed properties are *problem* properties. So unless you welcome solving problems while you earn *Big Money,* stay away from distressed properties.

When you take over any distressed property you may have to:

• Repair, rebuild, re-condition
• Re-paint, re-pave, re-roof
• Drain, dredge, dry
• Find new tenants; eject current tenants
• Raise rents; lower rents

So you see, distressed properties not only have built-in problems. They also require a large amount of work on *your* part. Of course, you can hire people to do this work for you. But when you first start, you may not have the cash needed to hire the people you need. So keep in mind—at all times—the Hicks rules for distressed properties:

1. It will always cost you *more* than you think it will to make big money from distressed property.
2. It will always take you *longer* to make money from distressed property than you think it will.

With these two rules in mind, you'll be able to face realistically the everyday problems that occur in the buying, selling, and running of distressed properties.

## HOW TO CONVERT DISTRESS INTO PROFITS

The keys to making money in any kind of distressed property are:

1. Buy cheap
2. Improve at low cost
3. Sell high

Now distressed properties are ideal for the Beginning Wealth Builder (BWB) because they can be bought either for *zero cash* or just a few hundred dollars. With such a small investment—or no investment at all—you can easily afford the *fix-up money* needed. "But," you say, "how can I afford the fix-up money when I have a poor credit rating, no money in the bank and three sick relatives to support?" Here's your answer, friend.

## BUILD A PAPER ROAD TO YOUR WEALTH

Let's say that the above conditions—or even *worse* ones—apply to you. Is the world still black, with all hope of a fortune for you lost forever? No, good friend, the money desires you have *can* be turned into sweet, green cash. And here's how.

Let's say you take over a distressed property worth $20,000 for *no* cash down. The property is a three-family house having an average rental of $150 per month per apartment, or a total of 3 x $150 = $450 per month. This gives you a yearly income of 12 x $450 = $5,400.

You survey the neighborhood and conclude that each apartment should be renting for at least $225 per month. Since there are no rent controls in the area, you raise the rents immediately. The tenants grumble a little but know that they're getting a bargain. So they agree to pay the higher rent. This means that your income jumps to 3 x 12 x $225 = $8,100 a year.

Using this as your rental income, and your ownership of the building as collateral, you go to your friendly bank and within one day borrow $5,000 for property improvement. While you're applying for the loan you're delighted to note that, just as Ty Hicks has told you in many of his other money books (which are listed at the beginning of *this* book), the bank loan officer:

- Hardly asked you *any* questions
- Was *delighted* to get your business
- Wanted to *lend* you more than you needed
- *Asked* you to hurry back for more money!

Thus, you've started your paper road to wealth, using sweet-smelling green-backs.

## CONVERT OWNERSHIP TO FUTURE INCOME

Next you take $3,000 of your borrowed $5,000 OPM (Other People's Money) and:

- Have the apartments painted
- Fix up leaks, broken windows, etc.
- Have the exterior spruced up

*Note: Pay* to have this work done. Don't do it yourself unless you're a first-rate mechanic!

With the building nice and shiny, you go back to the bank and tell your good friend that you'd like to refinance the mortgage—that is, get a new mortgage for 15 to 20 years. He sends an appraiser around to look at the building while you prepare a simple financial statement for the building. (I've prepared one for you and shown it in Fig. 1. You can use this as a general guide.)

Your friendly appraiser sets a fair value of $35,000 on your improved property—for which you put up no cash. And your friend at the bank tells you that the bank will lend you 80% of the appraised value of the property, or 0.80 ($35,000) = $28,000 instantly. Or, he says, you can easily get an FHA 90% guarantee, giving you $31,500. This will take a little longer—say 4 weeks.

### GET YOUR MONEY WHILE YOU CAN

You decide to *mortgage out* fast. So you accept the bank's $28,000 mortgage. You owe $20,000 on the building—that is, the price you "paid" for it. Since the mortgage gives you $28,000, you mortgage out with $28,000 - $20,000 = $8,000, less your closing costs of about $1,000. Thus, you net out with $7,000 cash, tax-free!

"But I still owe that $5,000 I borrowed to fix the place up," you say. True. But you used only $3,000 of that. Remember? So you have $9,000 cash and owe $5,000, or a net of $4,000.

Yet several other *nice* things have happened to you since you mortgaged out. These are:

a. Your mortgage payments are probably lower because you *extended* your mortgage.
b. Your *spendable* cash (also called MIF = money-in-fist) has increased because your mortgage payments are lower.
c. Your net worth has *risen* by $35,000, the appraised value of your property.
d. You converted your no-cost signature to *cash* without putting up a cent!

### BUILD YOUR REAL ESTATE EMPIRE

You now are in a good position to start building big real estate wealth because you have:

- Cash in your hand
- A steady income
- Property in *your* name

With these assets you're ready to go on to greater things—namely:

- More cash
- More income
- More property
- Without putting up more cash of your own!

This is how you build *your* real estate empire.

To start your empire:

1. Find another profitable rental property
2. Try to get this second property with *no* cash down
3. If you must put cash down, use the cash from mortgaging out on the first property
4. Or borrow the down payment using the first property as full or partial collateral for the down-payment loan
5. Once you take over the second property, try to mortgage out on it, just the way you did on the first property
6. Continue in this way until you have enough properties to give you the monthly income you seek

### KNOW THE NUMBERS OF EMPIRE BUILDING

Let's say that the average yearly income from each property you take over is $5,000, after all expenses are paid. This is a rather low annual income but it will give you a good idea of how the dollars can mount up. We'll say that you own different numbers of rental properties, and that each of them returns you $5,000 a year in profits, or:

| Number of Properties | Your Yearly Profit |
|---|---|
| 1 | $ 5,000 |
| 2 | 10,000 |
| 5 | 25,000 |
| 10 | 50,000 |
| 15 | 75,000 |
| 20 | 100,000 |
| 100 | 500,000 |

And, good friend, 100 properties is *not* a large number of properties to own *and* manage. Just think what you could do with an extra $500,000 *profit* every year of your life! You could live the "Golden Rule," namely: *"The guy or gal with the gold makes the rules."*

## FIX UP RUN-DOWN PROPERTIES FOR PROFIT

Real estate of all kinds goes through six stages in its life, namely:

1. New and shiny
2. Good-looking but not so new
3. Weathered but solid
4. Neglect beginning
5. Major repairs needed
6. Ready to be torn down

A new property is often worth 30% more the day it is finished than it cost to build. Thus, you'll often find that the following is true:

| Cost to Build | Value on Day Finished |
|---|---|
| $      20,000 | $      26,000 |
| 50,000 | 65,000 |
| 100,000 | 130,000 |
| 500,000 | 650,000 |
| 1,000,000 | 1,300,000 |
| 5,000,000 | 6,500,000 |
| 10,000,000 | 13,000,000 |

On the day the property is finished it is new and shiny, or in condition (1). From this condition to condition (3), *weathered but solid,* the value of your property will gradually increase because:

- Inflation is usually pushing property values up, money values down
- Labor and material costs usually are constantly rising (about 1% per month!)
- Land gets scarcer and scarcer, causing its value to rise (usually 15% per year!)
- Good properties are almost always in demand by someone for some purpose

But when *neglect begins,* condition (4), the building value often starts to decrease. Why? Because the fix-up costs begin to work *against* the increase in value. So from condition (4) through condition (6) you can often get valuable property for a song–*if you're willing to fix it up yourself, or pay someone else to fix it up.*

When you're starting with no cash, as many BWBs are, your sweat equity, or the work you do yourself on a property, can put you in the chips when you:

- Sell the property, or
- Borrow on the property, or
- Rent the property, or
- Trade for a better property

But you have to be a special type of person to make money this way. Why? Because:

- Not everyone is a good mechanic
- Some people aren't healthy enough
- Time may not be available
- Other work may be more interesting

Knowing that these conditions may exist in your life can really pay off. Why? Because you can decide to have someone else do the fixing up for you, paying for the repair work by using borrowed money. True, the repairs will cost you more this way but you'll have:

- More time for other work
- Less physical strain
- Fewer wealth-building problems

### PICK YOUR APPROACH TO FIX-UPS

There are three basic approaches to fixing up run-down properties:

1. Start small; grow big slowly
2. Start with six or eight buildings
3. Begin with a very large project and go all out

If you've never had any previous experience with fixing up buildings, I strongly suggest that you start with approach No. 1.

This way you can't go too far wrong if you find that you don't like making money from fix-ups. And if you like the fix-up approach, you can always expand quickly to take over other buildings. This is the way most folks start and move into the big money. Here's a typical example of how one BWB did it.

### Spare-Time Wealth In Fix-Ups

Glen T. is a typical white-collar worker—underpaid, under-appreciated, misunderstood, and over-bossed. Also, he's best at a desk instead of at a workbench or lathe. So when he first heard of big money to be made in fix-ups he turned away because of his poor mechanical ability. Yet the more he thought about the unhappiness on his job, the more Glenn felt that the fix-up route to real estate wealth might be his answer. He decided to take the big leap.

Glenn started with a two-family *repossession*—that is, a house that the bank had taken back (repossessed). The bank didn't ask for any cash down and arranged to have its lawyer handle the closing free of charge. So Glenn was able to take over a property for zero cash down. But the property:

- Had *no* tenants
- Was badly run down
- Needed many repairs
- Seemed ready for the house wrecker

But a bored man such as Glenn is also a desperate and "hungry" man. And desperation will often drive us to take action which we might not take otherwise.

Once Glenn had the house, he offered a contractor half the future rental income and half the profit on the sale of the property if the contractor would make the repairs free of charge. The contractor turned him down. So Glenn tried a second, then a third, and a fourth contractor, using the Yellow Pages of the phone book as his source of names. The eleventh contractor Glenn asked finally agreed to do the work.

Once the building was repaired and repainted, Glenn had no trouble renting both apartments. Thus, Glenn had gone from a condition of *no* property to the *owner* of *income-producing property* without investing anything other than:

- Some time
- Some energy
- His signature on a few papers

Sensing that his fortune wasn't far away, Glenn began buying repossessions all over town—*with no cash down.* In a year Glenn took over 33 multiple-family dwellings. In the same time he raised his assets from zero to some $65,000.

During his second year Glenn did much the same, taking over zero-cash properties in his own city and in nearby ones. By the end of the second year, Glenn's assets had risen to $480,000.

Glenn's third year was his big one because it was during this year that he began to trade his improved properties for bigger, newer buildings. When he closed out his third year Glenn was worth over $1-million—$1,072,000 to be exact!

You can do the same by wheeling and dealing in fix-ups. Just start, using the above ideas and you'll soon be in the big money!

## RUN MOTELS WITH ABSENTEE MANAGEMENT

Motels attract many BWBs because a motel seems to promise:

- Large, steady cash income
- Several sources of income—room rental, restaurant, bar, catering, etc.
- Steady increase in land and structure values
- Interesting and new people every day
- Relaxed working atmosphere

All these features of motels are true and accurate for modern motels which are well managed. But all motels have certain disadvantages, including:

- Motels are a 7-day-a-week business
- Most motels are a 365-day-a-year business
- Labor costs tend to be high in motels
- Labor problems can lead to headaches
- "Skips" or no-pay customers can cause income losses
- Expansion of your business may be impossible in crowded areas

Is there any way to get around these disadvantages? Yes, there is—at least in part. Why do I say in part? Because the famous Ty Hicks' law says:

There is *no perfect business!* Every business has problems of some kind. If you buy, start, or take over a business which earns you a profit, you are *certain* to have problems of some kind!

And what's the way *you* can partially get around the disadvantages of motels? There's a relatively simple answer—use a resident or local manager who will allow *you*—the owner—to operate by *absentee management.* In motel ownership, absentee management means that *you* don't have to be around the place seven days a week. *You* may even be able to run the motel profitably by spending only one hour a week on the premises!

## HOW TO MAKE BIG MONEY FROM MOTELS

You can make *big money* in motels if you:

- Run your motel as a sideline business
- Have a manager who takes care of day-to-day details
- Keep tight financial control
- Cater to lucrative customers
- Watch *all* your expenses
- Hold labor costs down

Let's look at the resident or local manager aspect because—to me—this is the most important feature of absentee management of motels. With this look I think you'll soon see that *you can make big money in motels.*

Who makes a good motel manager? My wide experience in this field shows that:

- Married men
- In their forties
- Who are ex-servicemen
- With kitchen or hospital experience
- Wanting to settle down
- Make excellent motel managers

Other good candidates for the job of motel manager include ex ship stewards, former hotel waiters, bartenders, and similar people. Why do I suggest married men with these backgrounds? Because:

The married man who has professional kitchen, catering, hospital, or similar experience can quickly learn all he needs to know about motel operation.

And, of course, being married gives the man greater stability and dependability than a single man. Also, by raising the man's salary by a few dollars a month, you can get his wife to help with certain jobs, like:

- Registering guests
- Supervising the housekeeping staff
- Hiring new maids, waitresses, and clerks
- Watching over the kitchen, if your motel has a restaurant

Yes, hiring the *right* manager can allow you the freedom you deserve and seek in your business life. Why? Because while you're operating your motel by absentee management, you can be:

- Building another business
- Searching for financing, new partners, or other assistance you might need
- Or just taking life easy!

### HOW ABSENTEE MANAGEMENT CAN PAY OFF

Let's say you take over a $400,000 motel with the following financing:

$300,000 first mortgage from a local bank
$125,000 second mortgage from the seller

You get $425,000 in financing but the motel cost you only $400,000. This means that you have $25,000 tax-free cash for:

- Closing costs
- Miscellaneous expenses
- Capital for buying another business
- Money to pay off existing debts

You take over the motel and have $17,000 left after paying your closing costs and some other small expenses that piled up during the past few months before you found this deal.

The average monthly profit on this motel when run by the owner and his wife is $8,000, or about $2,000 a week, after paying *all* expenses. You decide that you and your wife would prefer to be married to each other instead of to a motel. So, to "divorce" yourself from the motel, you decide to hire a competent manager.

After doing some figuring you decide that it would be worth $1,000 a month, plus an apartment in your motel for you to be free of 7-day-a-week slavery. Checking around, you quickly find that there are many good managers available for the pay you offer.

### START ON THE RIGHT BASIS

You advertise for a manager and interview more than a dozen. When you finally select your man you carefully outline his duties, both in spoken words and in writing, detailing:

- Work hours and work days
- Duties while on the job
- Pay schedule and pay benefits
- Annual vacation allowance
- Emergency procedures
- Other important job facts

With these facts presented to your prospective employee, he has a better chance of deciding if he'll like your job offer. And you have a better chance of deciding if you'll like him!

### FREEDOM CAN BE CHEAP

Now just look at what you're buying for $1,000 a month, plus an apartment. You'll have:

- Five days a week off
- Time to check out other businesses
- Freedom to travel
- Avoidance of drudgery

While you may think that giving up $1,000 a month, plus the apartment rent, is a high price to pay, listen to Ty Hicks when he says:

> Freedom from routine drudgery can open up new wealth vistas to you, can make you more creative, and put big money into your pocket.

So—if you *can* afford to do so—run your motel by absentee management. The extra income and leisure you'll get will be well worth the price!

### RENT OFFICES TO THE POSTAL SERVICE

One of the steadiest bill payers in the world is the U.S. Postal Service. And with postal rates constantly on the rise, it looks as though this fine reputation for dependable bill paying will go on for a long, long time.

You can make big money in real estate by building and renting post offices to the Postal Service. Why is this so? Because:

> With a long-term lease of your property by an AAAA-rated tenant, you can sit back and collect your rent without lifting a finger.

Or—if you want to—you can take your lease to the bank and borrow against the future income. You won't be able to borrow the full amount of your future rent, of course. But you *can* borrow a large portion of it—say 80 percent, on the average.

For example, let's say that you have a 20-year lease for a post office. You go around to your friendly banker who loaned you 90 percent of the cost of building your post office building. You show him your lease which pays you $10,000 a month rent for 20 years. "How much can I borrow on this lease?" you ask. "Sit down and we'll figure it out," he replies. He then writes out this column of figures:

| Year No. | Percent Loanable | Amount Loanable, $ |
|----------|------------------|--------------------|
| 1 | 100% | $120,000 |
| 2 | 95% | 114,000 |
| 3 | 90% | 108,000 |
| 4 | 90% | 108,000 |
| 5 | 90% | 108,000 |
| 6 | 85% | 102,000 |
| 7 | 85% | 102,000 |
| 8 | 80% | 96,000 |
| 9 | 80% | 96,000 |
| 10 | 75% | 90,000 |
| 11 through 20 | 70% | 84,000 a year |

For 20 years of regular rental of this property your income would be: (20 years) ($120,000 a year) = $2,400,000. But if you borrow against this income you will instantly receive $1,884,000—the sum of the above annual incomes. Then, as time passes, you will also receive an additional $516,000—the difference between the rent actually due you and the amount of money your bank loaned you. Of course, you'll have to pay interest on the money you borrowed. But—hopefully—you can put the money to work earning a higher rate of return than the interest you're paying!

## PUT YOUR OPM TO WORK

Your borrowed money is OPM—Other People's Money. You can take your $1.884-million and:

- Invest in other buildings
- Buy property for future development
- Take over a going business
- Set up other people in business
- Other

The big point here is that you can swing freely when you have cash in your pocket. Also, you've converted a long-term payout into instant money.

Can you work this deal with other types of tenants? You can—if they're AAA rated, or better. But keep these facts in mind:

- Different banks will offer different percentages on leases
- Tight-money times may cut your cash proceeds from a loan because the bank:

    (a) May not have much cash
    (b) May require that you leave 20% of the loan on deposit as a compensating balance

- Some banks may not want to lend on a lease

But never worry! If you look *long* enough, and *far* enough, you're certain to uncover a profitable loan deal for yourself. So don't give up—keep looking.

You *can* make money by using unusual real estate techniques. This chapter has mentioned a few unusual techniques you might want to consider using yourself. Why don't you sit down right now and list six more unusual techniques you might use in your local area? Your payoff could be in the millions!

### Points to Remember

- Unusual real estate wealth techniques can pay you millions in profits.

- Typical unusual real estate deals can be made in islands, view properties, distressed properties, motels, post offices, etc.
- OPM can get *you* started in unusual deals with zero cash.
- Run-down properties can be your fortune-maker.
- If you decide to invest in motels, be sure to use absentee management to save yourself from drudgery.

# 11

# BUILD REAL ESTATE PROFITS USING LIMITED PARTNERSHIPS

Real estate—in my opinion—is a beautiful business. Why? Because in real estate there are hundreds of chances for you to get started:

- In an activity that's an accepted "borrowing" business
- Without putting up a penny
- Using other people's money
- Keeping control of the deal
- In a hurry

And one of the best ways for you to consider getting started on zero cash without giving up control of your ideas and income sources is to use the *limited partnership* (L-P). Let's see how *you* can use this form of business to make your real estate fortune sooner.

## UNDERSTAND THE LIMITED PARTNERSHIP

Any partnership consists of two or more people who've joined together to do business. You're familiar—I'm sure—with many such partnerships. You'll often find lawyers working together in a partnership. The same is true of accountants, and some medical doctors.

In the usual partnership, each partner has an equal say in the management of the business. And should the business be sued, each partner has equal liability for debts, court awards, etc.

With such an arrangement, each equal partner is called a *general partner*. A partnership can—in most states—have as many general partners as it wants or needs.

Partnerships of all types are used in real estate activities. But in recent years the limited partnership has become very popular because it:

- Makes raising money easier
- Is easy to sell to the "public"
- Gives good control of the business

In a limited partnership you may have two or more *general* partners and a large number of *limited partners*. Your limited partners:

- Have *no* voice or vote in the management of the partnership
- Are limited in their liability—in case of a lawsuit—to the amount of money they put into the partnership—usually $5,000, $10,000, or more, per limited partner
- May obtain major tax advantages from being limited partners

### WHAT THE L-P OFFERS INVESTORS

"Why," you ask, "do people put their money into (invest in) limited partnerships?" There are a number of reasons, each of which is important to *you*, if you plan to use the L-P as a source of money for building your real estate riches. Thus, people invest in L-Ps to:

- Earn real estate profits without the daily operating headaches
- Save taxes on other income
- Earn future capital-gain profits
- Keep their excess funds working for them

While you may not believe this, there are millions of people in this great country of ours who are looking for good, profitable real estate deals into which they can put their money. And if you can put one or more good deals together you can get the money you need to:

- Build new structures
- Fix up existing properties
- Buy profitable properties
- Manage profitable properties

Better yet, you don't have to put up a cent of your own. And you can get the real estate funds you need:

- Without registering stock
- Without complicated legal documents
- Quickly, easily, and at low cost

Let's see how you can get your L-P going.

## HOW TO FORM YOUR L-P

To form a L-P you *must* have the guidance of an attorney. So what I tell you here is done with the understanding that you—as an intelligent Beginning Wealth Builder (BWB)—will have the good sense to see an attorney *before* you actually form your L-P. However, you will probably find that your attorney agrees with much that is said here. And if he's unfamiliar with L-Ps, he may find the following facts a useful introduction.

To form your L-P, without having to register it with the Federal Government[1], take these 7 lucky steps:

1. Decide that you will be one of the *general partners*
2. Select one or more other general partners
3. Pick the number of limited partners you'd like to have (usually 10 to 20, depending on the amount of money you need and the price per participation)
4. Prepare, or have prepared, the L-P description
5. Sell or have someone else sell, the participation units
6. Invest the proceeds in the real estate activity for which the L-P was formed
7. Go out and earn those profits you planned on!

These steps give you the simplest and least complicated kind of L-P because you usually need not register it (under present laws)

---

[1] You may, however, have to register with your State Government. Your attorney will advise you on this IMPORTANT matter.

with the Securities and Exchange Commission (SEC) of the United States Government. Later, when you gain more experience, you can sell thousands of participations, provided you conform to the proper SEC rules and regulations. But, for the moment, let's take a closer look at each of the steps you'll take in forming the simpler and smaller L-P, with the help of your attorney. (For, as I said earlier, you *must* have the help of an attorney when you form a L-P.)

## SELECT YOUR GENERAL PARTNER

To gain the maximum from your first L-P, I suggest that *you* become one of the general partners (GP). As a GP you'll get in on the financial and operating management of your L-P. This will teach you plenty about:

• Borrowing money
• Handling people
• Running a real estate business

So once you've appointed yourself a GP, pick at least one other GP. Note that by definition a partnership must have at least *two* members. And, of course, you can have many more, if you wish.

Pick your GP—and I suggest that you have only one GP for your first L-P venture—as carefully as you'd choose a:

• Wife
• Husband
• Doctor
• Lawyer
• Accountant

Why should you be so careful in picking your GP? Because the two of you will be working together for a year, or longer. You'll be sharing decisions, solving problems, and earning profits together. If you don't see eye-to-eye at the start, your partnership may wreck an otherwise perfect deal. I've seen it happen plenty of times.

To be certain you're picking a compatible, helpful partner for your real estate deal:

• Find out what your prospective GP can contribute to the partnership in:

Time
Money
Ideas
Energy

- Ask your partner-to-be what *he* or *she* wants out of the deal
- Then ask what *he* or *she* can give to the deal

My experience with many L-P shows that unless a prospective GP has something to *give* the L-P in terms of himself, he is usually an unsuitable candidate. So be careful—don't rush your GP choice.

## PICK THE NUMBER OF L-P

In most states you can have a *private* offering of partnership shares to *limited partners.* Such an offering *usually* need not be registered with Federal authorities if you sell 25, or fewer, participations, in one state. Some states require a simple registration of L-Ps with the County Clerk, Attorney General, or some similar official. A nominal fee (which varies from state to state) may also be charged for the registration. You can easily learn if registration of *your* L-P is required in *your* state by writing to the Attorney General for your state. Or your attorney can quickly answer the question.

So, to avoid the need for SEC registration of your L-P, offer 23 or fewer L-P participations to the residents of only *one* state, on a *private* (non-advertised) basis, where the limit of 25 applies. You may also be able to avoid the need for state registration by having a private offering to 23, or fewer, L-Ps. (I suggest 23 instead of 25 L-Ps just to keep you on the safe side. In some states you need not register a L-P if you have 50, or fewer, L-Ps). But *be sure to check this out with your attorney before you take any action to offer even one participation!*

## FIGURE YOUR CASH FLOW

Let's put *you* into a L-P real estate deal. You'd like to buy a two-year-old 250-unit rental building which is completely modern in every way—swimming pool, tenant garages, electronic security system, etc. The seller wants $550,000 cash down.

You negotiate with the seller, using the famous Hicks law of Real Estate Buying, namely:

Never pay the asking price on any piece of real estate. Always negotiate a lower price, particularly for the cash portion of the asking price.

You take this advice and go to work. Your hours of wheeling and dealing on the down payment are worthwhile. You get the cash down payment reduced from $550,000 to $470,000. Also, the seller agrees to share the closing costs, which you figure will run some $50,000.

Everything else about the deal is good—that is, the place will throw off a big cash flow to the investors, and you and they will have a sweet tax shelter in the form of depreciation. Here are the figures:

| | |
|---|---|
| Annual income | $ 750,000 |
| Total price | $3,800,000 |
| Cash down | $ 470,000 |

With these figures in mind, you aim to put together a L-P to:

1. Finance the down payment
2. Operate the building
3. Earn a profit from the building

## PUT YOUR L-P TOGETHER

You need a total cash down payment of $470,000, plus $25,000 for your share of the closing costs, plus an emergency fund of $5,000, or a total of $500,000. Knowing that you want to make a *private offering*, to avoid registration, you limit your L-P to 20 limited partners. This means that each limited partner will have to put in at least $500,000/20 = $25,000. And, if you can get more, say $28,000 from each limited partner, you will try to do so!

You and your other *general partner* will manage the property. So you put up *no* cash—instead you sign an agreement to run the building for a stated period, or until the property is sold. (If you wanted to, of course, you *could* put up whatever cash in multiples of $25,000 which you could afford. But I'm trying to show you how to work out a L-P on *zero cash*.)

With your plans set, you write a L-P description or prospectus. To help you, you'll find a sample L-P description included in the

IWS "Starting Millionaire" Program. You may want to use this as a guide. Or you may want to change it completely. Either way, however, it will give you a starting point. Or it may help your attorney get started on writing the description for you. (You can order the "Starting Millionaire" Program from IWS Inc., Bank Plaza, Merrick, NY 11566, for $99.50.) You can benefit from a quick reading of the L-P description given in this Program. Why? Because it shows you what information such a description usually contains. Also, since this description is for a real estate L-P, you can get a good start on what kind of data you'll have to get for the description of *your* L-P.

So have your attorney write the description of your L-P as soon as you have enough facts. Or write the description yourself and give it to your attorney for editing and polishing up. Once you have your L-P description written, you've "put the deal together" on paper. (And writing the description will have been a wonderfully enlightening experience for you!)

Now you have to find enough limited partners with enough money to make the deal go!

## WHERE TO FIND LIMITED PARTNERS

If you have a whole string of rich friends, you'll have little trouble in getting the money you need from them. But if you don't have many (or *any*) rich friends, as is the case with most BWBs, you'll have to:

- Find L-Ps yourself
- Get friends to recommend L-Ps
- Use any other available sources of L-Ps such as ads in the monthly newsletter *International Wealth Success*

Let's take a look at each of these potential sources of L-Ps.

### Find L-Ps Yourself

Most L-Ps are wealthy people seeking the pluses of real estate investing without any of the drawbacks, other than the remote chance of losing some tax-deductible dollars. So you have to locate such people from local sources like:

- A social register
- Lists of golf and country club members

- Expensive-auto dealer lists
- County Clerk lists of investors in other limited partnerships
- Rentable mailing lists of high-income people

Before approaching any of these people *be certain to get the advice of your attorney!*

### Get Help From Friends

If you have wealthy friends, they may be able to give you the names of other wealthy people who might be interested in buying participations in your L-P. And if you do not have wealthy friends, as is probably the case, you'll have to try to meet some rich people.

You can meet wealthy people in the places they usually go—such as:

- Golf Clubs
- Country clubs
- Yacht clubs
- University and college clubs
- Expensive restaurants
- Other similar places

The advantages of meeting wealthy people are often overlooked by the not-so-wealthy. These advantages include:

- Most wealthy people are relaxed and friendly. Why? Because it's easy to be nice when you have a wad of money in the bank!
- One wealthy contact can lead to ten or more others.
- Once you make money for one wealthy person your reputation will spread to hundreds of others—they'll be "throwing money in your face," trying to get you to invest it for them.

So cultivate *every* wealthy person you meet. You can benefit enormously from the contacts you make. (As an aside, make a habit of being friendly with everyone. You'll be happier—and you'll make many other people happy. Also, you will eventually profit from such an outlook).

### Use Other Available Sources

To get started in any business you usually have to spend money. As the man said: "It takes money to make money!"

But where does a BWB turn when he has little, or no, money to spend on the advertising he wants to do to attract investors in a real estate project? One place he can turn to is the monthly newsletter *International Wealth Success*. Costing only $24 a year for a full 12-issue subscription, this helpful publication gives you: 100%, 110%, 115% financing (money) sources; compensating-balance loan sources; new wealth ideas every month; many, many sources of business loans; part-time money-making ideas; mail-order riches opportunities; hundreds of finders fee listings; world-wide international money-making ideas; fast-fortune easy-money wealth deals; franchise riches ideas and methods; capital available for borrowers of many types; monthly Ty Hicks page where Ty talks to you; financial broker opportunities; hundreds of other ideas, sources and ways to earn big money and make your fortune today; ways to get money you need; unique techniques to earn big money; secrets that put cash into your pocket.

### APPROACH PROSPECTS CAREFULLY

You are making a *private* offering of your L-P. So you must be very careful not to violate any SEC or State rules and regulations. I can't act as your partnership advisor in this book. And I don't intend to try to so act. Only your *attorney* can do so. But in any private offering of a L-P you *must* be careful to:

- Follow *ALL* SEC and State requirements
- Limit your offer to the number and resident limitations for your area
- Prepare a suitable description (often called a prospectus) for your offer (your attorney can do this, if you can't)
- Be factual and accurate in ALL your dealings

### SELL YOUR PARTICIPATIONS; START WORKING

Returning to the L-P we were considering above, let's see how it stands. With your 20 prospects identified and contacted, you sell each one a participation for $28,000, a price that is acceptable to all.[2] The L-P thus takes in $560,000 in cash. Each limited partner signs the necessary forms, as shown in the L-P offering mentioned earlier in this chapter.

With this cash in hand you negotiate the deal and take over the rental property for which the L-P was formed. As a general partner you get a negotiated income which is acceptable to you. Also, you may get a portion of the ownership in the property, depending on the deal you worked out. As you get the various aspects of the property organized the way you want them, you can begin thinking of your *next* L-P.

## BUILD YOUR FUTURE RICHES

By assembling a series of L-Ps, you can easily build a million-dollar real estate fortune in a few years. And as each L-P grows and earns money for its members, you'll find you can sell participations quicker and with less effort. Why? Because your reputation will spread rapidly amongst monied people. Soon they'll be begging you to sell them participations—sight unseen!

Yes, the real estate L-P *can* be *your* road to future riches. But to use this way to *your* wealth, you *must* have the advice of an attorney. Don't try to do it yourself—you can wind up with all kinds of legal problems which can eat away your profits—both present and future.

### Points to Remember

- A limited partnership can build your real estate wealth fast.
- You *must* have a competent attorney to advise you in any limited partnership.
- Be sure to follow all national and local laws when setting up and running your limited partnership.

---

[2] This $28,000 is a higher partnership price YOU worked out with each prospect to give the L-P more starting cash. (No L-P was ever hurt—that I know of—by some extra starting cash!)

# 12

## GO THE CONDO ROUTE TO YOUR REAL ESTATE WEALTH

Real estate wealth builders are amongst the most creative folks I've ever known. And—friend—I've met thousands of wealth builders in many parts of this great world of ours. So you'll find—when you meet them—that real estate people are dedicated, creative, ambitious, alert, and enterprising folk.

### SEE ZERO CASH AT WORK

Real estate people invented the condominium—*condo* for short—because they felt a need to satisfy the man and woman in the street who enjoys living in an apartment house and who is seeking:

- A piece of real estate of their own
- Legal tax deductions for their real estate
- A "piece of the action" in real estate property price rises
- Superior housing or office space

In a condo each owner has all the above advantages. And the real estate wealth builder—yourself—gets the *big* return which can be earned by someone using his or her brain and creative thinking. Let's see how you can put zero cash to work in condos.

## WATCH YOUR WEALTH GROW

Let's say that you spot a nice piece of land for an income apartment house. You make a quick survey of the property-and find that you can put up a 100-unit building at an average cost of $15,000 per unit, including the purchase of the land. This means that the total cost of your income building will be: 100 units x $15,000 per unit = $1,500,000. With the usual real estate financing, you can borrow up to 70% of this amount or 0.70 x $1,500,000 = $1,050,000. So, to construct this building on this land, you'll have to raise $1,500,000 - $1,050,000 = $450,000 cash.

But if you decide to make the building a condo and *sell* each of the 100 apartments, here's what happens:

- The land cost remains the *same*
- The construction cost remains the *same*
- Your borrowing ability *zooms*

Let's see how this can happen. You'll quickly see the value of creative financing using *none* of your own cash.

## PUT OPM TO WORK NOW

A condo apartment will usually command a list price of at least twice its cost. This means that the apartments in this building will sell for $30,000. (Your asking price would probably be $29,995). Thus, your potential revenue from selling 100 apartments would be: 100 units x $30,000/unit = $3,000,000. With a 70% loan-to-value ratio, as before, you can borrow 0.70 x $3,000,000 = $2,100,000. Since the building and land will cost you $1,500,000, you could (with the figures we have here) *mortgage out* with $2,100,000 - $1,500,000 = $600,000 cash!

"But," you say, "I can get 70% financing for a rental-income building I can put up on this land. Won't that change the deal?" No, I reply, it really won't change it that much because you'll still have to come up with cash for the rental building (30% of $1,500,000, or $450,000 here) while you'd net out with MIF (money in fist) on the condo. True, it is usually easier to rent an apartment than to sell one, but the whole point is:

With a condo you can often get 100+% financing from the start.
But this is often difficult with a straight rental building.

## LEARN THE FACTS OF REAL ESTATE MONEY

"But why," you ask, "can I get such a better deal on the
condo?" There are several reasons. These include:

- With the condo, you sell out all (or almost all) of your
  ownership of the property
- You have little rise in value of your condo building because
  you don't own much (or any) of it
- Rise in land values are also out for you for the same reason

So—if you want to go the cash-on-the-line route—pick the
conventional rental building deal, either residential or commercial.
But if you're the Beginning Wealth Builder (BWB) I think you
*might* be, with:

- Little cash today
- No big inheritances coming along
- Possible credit problems
- Strapped for future loans

then the condo way to wealth is a great way to start. (For even if
you never put up your own condo, you'll learn a great deal just by
checking out the condo idea).

## CONDOS ARE BUSTING OUT ALL OVER

Recently I made a wonderful cross-country editorial and business trip, stopping along the way to visit many readers of my
books and my *International Wealth Success* newsletter. While on
this trip I was delighted to see how widely condos had caught on
because I saw:

- Town-house type condos
- Apartment-house type condos
- Office-building condos
- Industrial-park condos

"Why," you ask, "are so many condos being put up?" I'm glad
you asked, I reply. Here are a few of the more important reasons
for putting up so many condos:

- 100%, or better, financing is often possible
- The land gets "higher use" because the structure on it is worth more
- Less time may be needed for the financing approval
- Condos sell faster because they help people and firms make tax savings

Truly, good BWB friend, the condo concept could put you into the millionaire class sooner than you think! And I'd just love to see you in that class within the next year—or even sooner.

## PLAY THE CONDO GAME ON ZERO CASH

As many of you who've read my earlier books, taken my courses, or read my newsletter know, I'm a *zero-cash* enthusiast from way back. By this I mean:

> It is my firm belief—based on years of actual experience—that you can start, and succeed in, your own business, using very little, or no cash at all!

And condos are one zero-cash activity in which you can "get off the ground" quickly and easily. Let's see how.

Two friends of mine moved south recently and soon discovered the condo boom in their new city. Seeing condo apartments advertised for *no cash down* while still in the construction stage, they "bought" several of these condos by just signing a few papers. Since it would take at least a year for the condo to be finished, these friends thought there was a good chance that the value of each apartment would increase and they could sell out their options at a profit.

And that's just what happened! Each friend realized a $2,500 profit on each apartment in less than a year without investing a penny!

Other people use a similar method for condo apartments requiring a fully-refundable down payment. They hold the apartment until they sell the option. Or—if they can't sell the option—they allow the apartment to revert to the building promoter and get a full refund of their money. Their only loss is the interest the money might have earned for them if they left it in the bank. Deposits required for condos under construction are often nominal—$100 or thereabouts. Some developers, however, may require you to deposit $3,000, or more.

There are other ways of playing the condo game on zero cash. These include:

1. Taking over several units in a condo with no cash down by using your relatives and friends. Arrange the order each person gives so that you cover the most desirable areas in the building—such as corners, top floor, penthouse, or any other areas you think will be popular. Sell out these holdings as the demand for space in the building increases. Hold choice spots until the end, when the prices are likely to be highest.

2. Offer to help sell units for the owner, provided he gives you title to one or more units for no cash down. Hold your units until the last and then *sell out* at a high price.

Before using any of these methods, be sure to check them out with your attorney. The rules on condos vary widely from one state to another. You *must* obey the laws in force in your state.

## USE THE "NEW" CONDO METHODS

As I mentioned earlier, real estate people are amongst the most creative folks I've ever met. So—a few months ago—when I first heard of the "new" condo I was delighted to see that it was another example of creative real estate thinking. Here's how it works.

In many cities some of the older apartment houses and office buildings have—in recent years—been owned by their owners for so long that they have ceased to provide tax shelter. This means that much of the income from the building is taxable, leaving fewer money-in-fist (MIF) spendable dollars. So some of the owners decided they wanted "out." To get out some owners hit on the idea of selling the building to the rent-paying tenants! Here's how this works.

Let's say that you own a 10-unit building having ten identical units. The building and land are worth a total of $100,000. You decide you want to sell the building to the tenants.

With a value of $100,000 for the land and the building and 10 units in the building, each unit is—at first glance—worth $100,000/10 units = $10,000.

But let's look at your building a little closer. When a tenant buys a unit (which is his complete apartment plus part of the lobby, land, etc.) he gets:

- Ownership of his unit
- Tax deductions he may not have had before
- Part ownership of the land
- A chance to get in on the rise in value of the property
- Other benefits of ownership

So—you say—each unit is really worth more than $10,000. Every unit is worth—in your opinion—$15,000. You propose to the tenants that the building be converted to a condo (after you've had your attorney advise you on the legal aspects in *your* area). Six tenants agree right off. Four tenants refuse.

Depending on the area your property is in, you can start converting right away. (The rules vary from one area to another, so *check with your attorney*).

Let's say that you sell six units within a month for $15,000 each, giving you $90,000 cash. You then still own 40 percent of the building.

Two of the four tenants who refused your condo idea soon move out in disgust. You quickly sell these two units and you now have $90,000 + $30,000 = $120,000 in cash and you still own 20 percent of a $100,000 building!

Now, you can easily sell out the other two units. Or you can keep one for yourself and sell out the other. If you do this you'll come out of the deal with $135,000 in cash and a 10 percent ownership in the building!

## GET IN ON THE "NEW" CONDO YOURSELF

"Ty," you say, "this is a great idea! There's just one catch, man—*I don't have any building to sell to the tenants*. Further, I *don't* even have the cash to get the building to sell to the tenants! So your idea is a bad one for me."

"Now hold on a moment," I reply. Recall that real estate is:

- A borrowed-money business
- Often a 100% + financed business
- A business with billions in lendable cash
- A business in which beginners can win riches

Being interested in a borrowed-money business can really make your life much easier. Why? Because it means that:

- There's money available for *you*
- This money is easier to get
- You can probably get 100% + financing

Let's see how the "new" condo could work for you.

Let's say you see an older office building in your area which you'd like to buy and convert to a commercial condo. The price of the building and land is $500,000. You think you can convert the building to a condo and get $700,000 to $800,000 for it. Let's trace the steps you take.

### Find the Mortgage Data You Need

In any real estate deal, your initial step, after learning the price of the property you want, is to find out:

a. The first mortgage amount, if any, on the property
b. The amount of any junior mortgages (2nd, 3rd, 4th, etc.) on the property

Once you have the mortgage data, your next steps are:

a. Determine if you can assume (take over) the existing mortgage
b. If you can't take over the existing mortgage, determine how large a new first mortgage you can get on the property
c. Find out how large a purchase-money mortgage (PM) the seller will give you

Using the above steps, you find out that you cannot take over the existing first mortgage. This often happens when the interest rate on the existing mortgage is two or three percentage points below the going interest rates on mortgages at the time you want to buy the property.

While asking about the existing mortgage you also learn that you can get a new mortgage for 70% of the property value, or 0.70 x $500,000 = $350,000. This means that—if you want to take over the property for 100+% financing, and we're assuming you do—you'll have to find $500,000 - $350,000 = $150,000 for the junior mortgages. Also, your closing costs (legal fees, taxes, etc.), will probably run about $5,000.

Next, you ask about junior mortgages. (These are second, third, fourth, etc. mortgages). There are various ways you can get such mortgages. The ways used most often include:

1. Borrowing from a second-mortgage lender
2. Getting the seller to give you a mortgage for all, or part of the amount you need (This is called a purchase-money or PM mortgage)
3. A combination of these methods

You ask the seller to give you as large a PM mortgage as possible. He agrees to give you a PM mortgage of $50,000, leaving you with $150,000 - $50,000 = $100,000 still to go.

To get this $100,000 you contact a second mortgage lender. After some discussion he agrees to lend you $105,000, the $100,000 plus $5,000 for closing costs. The term or duration of your loan will be 5 years.

## TAKE OVER THE PROPERTY YOU WANT

You meet with your attorney, the seller, the mortgage lenders, and arrange for the *contract.* This is the usual first step in most real estate purchase deals. In the time between the contract and the closing (called the *passing* in some states), you get the various loans you need.

At the closing there's usually a mad shuffling of papers, a lot of talk in terms you may not understand, and the signing of what seems like hundreds of names on dozens of papers. But after a hectic 90 minutes you finally own your own office building! You're really in real estate—at long last.

True, you now owe various banks, people, and other lenders $500,000. But you *do* have an income to pay off these loans, plus depreciable property to shelter from taxes all—or almost all—of your income. And you have your plan to convert to a condo as soon as possible. Also, your assets have risen by half a million dollars! (So have your liabilities, or what you owe!)

## GET YOUR MONEY BACK QUICKLY

Once you have this office building in your own name, you approach the tenants either personally, by telephone, or by mail, asking them if they are interested in buying their rented space. As is usual when such requests are made, 50 to 60 percent probably say yes immediately. You sell their space to them and within three months you've taken in $573,000. You use this to pay off the various loans on the building.

Once you have some "financial breathing room"—that is you've either completely, or almost completely, paid off your loans—you can start concentrating on the last few tenants. In almost every condo conversion it's the sale of the property to these "end-of-the-line" tenants which puts the big-money profits into *your* pockets.

Selling out to these tenants brings in another $292,000. Here's how the over-all deal works out for you:

| | |
|---|---|
| Total selling price of condo | = $865,000 |
| Cost of property, including closing | = 505,000 |
| Gross income, excluding interest | = $360,000 |
| Interest, real estate taxes, miscellaneous | = 68,000 |
| Net profit | = $292,000 |

So—starting with *no* cash—you have, in a period of a few months, accumulated nearly $300,000. Of course, you'll have to pay income taxes on this profit. However, if you earn this much in a few months, I'm sure you'll be pleased to pay the taxes due.

## ANOTHER "NEW" CONDO IDEA

In some areas of the country which have vacation appeals—such as Florida, California, South Carolina, etc.—real estate wealth builders recently came up with another "new" condo idea. In this one, each of 6, or more, people buys a one-sixth (or less) interest in a condo apartment unit. Each buyer can spend 2 months of the year in his condo apartment. Or—if any buyer wishes—he or she can rent his or her apartment out for the two months, instead of living in it. By renting the apartment out for two months, the buyer can usually pay for it (that is, recover his or her investment) in 3 to 4 years.

Now what does this mean to *you*—a beginning real estate wealth builder offering such apartments for sale? Well, since you may have difficulty selling an apartment in times of reduced economic activity, this approach can get you your cash money inflow faster. Let's see how.

Say that you build or buy a building having 20 apartment units in a vacation area. Typical values of such vacation units are in the

$50,000 range—and higher. Using $50,000 each for your units, fully furnished, a 1/6 interest would cost a buyer $50,000/6 = $8,333. Besides his one-sixth ownership, the buyer will also get common ownership use of the building's recreational facilities, pool, dock, etc.

To you, as a condo real estate wealth builder, there are a number of big advantages in doing business this way, including.

- It is often easier to sell smaller priced partial units
- As soon as a portion of a unit is sold, cash becomes available to you
- You can earn fees handling the rental of the condos during the year

So, if you'd like to live in a vacation area, while you earn money, think about going the condo route—either full or partial! It might put *you* into the big money soon!

## CO-OPS ALSO MAKE MONEY

Cooperative real estate—often called co-ops—is probably more common for apartment houses than for any other type of real estate. In a co-op each tenant owns one or more shares of stock in a corporation which—in turn—owns the building and land. Ownership of one or more shares of stock entitles the tenant to occupy one apartment in the building. Monthly or annual maintenance charges are paid by each tenant for the upkeep of the building. The charge for maintenance is usually based on the area occupied by the tenant's apartment.

Since ownership in a co-op is shared, there is less chance for a Beginning Real Estate Wealth Builder to hit the big money. For this reason, most BWBs prefer the condo route to wealth.

But if you'd like to try to build your real estate wealth in co-ops, you might want to consider trying the following:

1. Use borrowed money to buy one or more co-op units
2. Become active in the co-op management group
3. Push the idea of constant improvement of the property by the management
4. If you own more than one unit, rent out the units you don't occupy yourself

5. Try to take over other units in the building so you share in more of the value rise
6. Sell out when prices reach a level where you can earn a good profit

### Points to Remember

- Condos offer owners a "piece of the real estate profit action."
- Condos offer greater profit potentials to many real estate operators.
- OPM (Other People's Money) is a powerful force in condo wealth building.
- 100% + financing *is* possible with condos.
- Condos are being built in many areas of the country and for many purposes.
- Some condos can be financed with "zero cash."
- Existing buildings are sometimes converted to condos by being sold to their tenants.
- Office and industrial buildings are now being built as, or converted to, condos.
- Junior mortgages can often help you get 100% financing of condos.
- Condos offer quick recovery of your cash investment.
- Vacation condos offer wealth opportunities to real estate wealth builders.
- Co-op buildings can also make money for some real estate dealers.

# 13

## HOW TO COMBINE REAL ESTATE AND OTHER PROFITABLE BUSINESSES

Many Beginning Wealth Builders (BWBs) I meet (and I meet many thousands) are more interested in earning *big* money from a business than from real estate. Yet when they try to borrow money for another business—say an indoor swimming pool, a boat marina, hardware store, etc.—they find the money is hard to raise. So when they hear of 100% financing in real estate, they find it difficult to believe. Yet—with a little thinking and planning—they might get 100% financing for the business they like when they combine it with real estate. Let's see how.

### GO THE BORROWED-MONEY ROAD

Ken P. is a swimming "nut." He swims every day of the year he can get near the water. (I think he even swims in his bathtub!) Besides swimming for exercise, Ken gives swimming lessons, teaches skin and scuba diving, and works as a lifeguard at a local beach. Ken's ambition in life—as you might guess—is to own an indoor swimming pool in which he can give year-round swimming lessons while taking a daily dip himself.

"I don't want to go into real estate," Ken told me on the phone one evening when he called me for help. "Yet when I try to borrow money to build an indoor pool people say: 'Come around *after* you've put up the pool and we'll be glad to help you then.'"

"Ken," I replied, "I've heard stories like this a hundred times. What you have to do is start using some creative financing methods!"

"But how can I use creative financing methods when I can't get the money to start with?" he asked. "You have to go the borrowed-money route," I replied. Then I pointed out to Ken that:

1. Real estate is a borrowed-money business.
2. An indoor swimming pool usually needs land and a building.
3. It is common practice to borrow money to buy land.
4. It is also common practice to borrow money to construct a building.
5. By thinking in terms of real estate instead of the business which will eventually occupy the real estate, the business person can often get 100% financing for both the real estate *and* the business.
6. Many businesses eventually earn more from their real estate investments than they do from their regular profit-making activities.

"Sounds good," Ken said. "But I don't want to be a miserable little landlord. I want to make big money so I can really enjoy my life!"

## GET ALL THE THINGS YOU WANT

Ken's remark about the "miserable little landlord" really annoyed me. "Ken," I said, "until you're ready to at least listen to what I say, you can try getting free help for yourself elsewhere." Then I hung up.

The reason I was annoyed was because I had just returned from a February Caribbean business trip to the beautiful island of Barbados. There I'd met one of the biggest real estate men in the world—a man who owned 14,000 rental apartments in a northern city of the United States.

During a friendly conversation in the gazebo overlooking the beautiful Caribbean palms, sand, and water, I did some quick mental arithmetic.

"With 14,000 units and an average monthly rent of $100 per unit, your monthly gross income is around $1,400,000," I said to the real estate man. And in 12 months you take in some $16,800,000. That's a nice piece of change to any business person."

He laughed. "It sure is! But your average rent figure is a bit low. My actual cash income the last time I looked—is about $18-million a year. It keeps me in Caddies and penthouses and big yachts without any problems!"

So this man was no "miserable little landlord." And he started by using borrowed money to take over his first property! Further, he built his empire on borrowed money! Yet, here was a BWB (Ken) with *no* money who was ready to criticize another class of business person without any real reason for doing so. Since I admire people who start with little and end up with a big bundle, I also try to protect them from critics who "shoot from the hip."

Ken—as you probably guessed—called back a few nights later, full of apologies. During our conversation I told him about my Barbados friend and his $18-million a year cash flow. "Now, Ken," I joked, "I know that $18-million a year isn't much money to *you*, but it sure is a lot to most people!"

Ken sputtered and said: "Stop the kidding and tell me how I can get started in real estate—tonight!" I answered Ken by telling him the steps usually taken by business people who combine real estate with another business are:

1. Decide what business you want to enter
2. Determine how much real estate you need
3. Look for a suitable property and building (if needed)
4. Get a price for the property from the seller
5. Borrow as much money as you need
6. Take over the property
7. Start running your business on the property

Ken took these steps. The only difference was that Ken had to have a suitable building put up for his swimming pool because none of the properties he found had a building he could use. Because his area needed a recreational facility as well as a pool, Ken added a gym, meeting rooms, a game room, and other facilities to his pool building—all on 100% financing.

Today Ken has a booming pool and recreation business. His customers include thousands of local residents—both men and women—and numerous local Boy Scout, Girl Scout, Sea Scout, and Explorer Scout troops, high-school and college swimming teams, etc.

Recently Ken gave me a guided tour of his pool, showing me the game room with its checker boards, billiard tables, ping-pong tables, and card tables. I also saw a big, well lighted gym crowded with teenage girls practicing in their black ballet jumpers. (Ken has found dance instruction to be a lucrative source of extra income.)

We also visited the spotless locker rooms, each equipped with modern showers and steam rooms. Mirrors covered many of the walls, giving a bright, clean appearance to the entire layout.

And—of course—the pool area is Ken's delight. There are really two pools—one for diving practice and contests and the other for swimming practice and contests. Done in modern decorative tile, the pools are the nicest I've ever seen anywhere.

"Ty," Ken said as we finished our tour, "I'm sorry for my crack about the landlord. You were right to hang up on me. It brought me to my senses. I have to thank real estate for putting me in the recreation business! Thanks again, friend."

## UNDERSTAND WHAT REAL ESTATE CAN DO FOR YOU

There are hundreds of other businesses which you can "hinge" and leverage around real estate. When I say hinge and leverage I mean:

> With a real estate-based business you can often borrow the money you need for the business and the real estate by using the real estate as the collateral for your loan.

Typical real estate-based businesses (that is, businesses in which real estate is an important element of the business profit activity) include:

- Marinas, boat yards
- Camps, hunting lodges, theme parks
- Mobile home parks, trailer parks
- Motels, hotels, youth hostels
- Apartment houses, condominiums

- Auto wrecking yards, junk yards
- Factories of many kinds
- Airports, golf courses, country clubs
- Parking lots, garages, storage yards
- Warehouses, mini-warehouses

There are many others.

Since a number of these businesses require little investment other than that for the real estate, you can often get started, or take over, a going business on little, or no, cash. This means that the real estate serves as your collateral or backing for the loan. While you may be much more interested in your business activities (such as a parking lot, a mobile home park, tennis court, etc.) than in real estate, it may be the land or buildings which put you into your business!

### HOW TO GET BUSINESS MONEY THROUGH REAL ESTATE

Since real estate is a borrowed-money business, it is usually much easier to borrow on real estate than on any other type of business. (Yes! Real estate *is* also a business). Knowing this, you can get ready to combine real estate and the business of your choice. For best results, you might want to consider taking these six profit-laden steps:

1. Try to keep your business cash needs as low as possible.
2. Allow time for your business to grow—don't expect the real estate to support gold-plated jet planes at the start!
3. Pay attention to the details of your real estate deals—they may make you a bigger fortune than your business does!
4. Try to get some monthly income from your real estate, besides using it as a source of 100% financing and a place to conduct your business.
5. Hold onto your real estate while prices are rising in your area.
6. Keep accurate records of your real estate expenses, income, and profits.

In most businesses, real estate—either rented or owned—is just an extra expense we have to pay. What I'm suggesting here is that you make this extra-expense item pay for itself and, hopefully, earn *you* a profit.

### RENTED PROPERTY CAN EARN YOU BIG PROFITS

A young friend of mine is a world-recognized computer expert. His firm grew quickly from a borrowed desk in a friend's office to a payroll of more than 100 people because he worked hard and gave good service to his customers. After several expansions of his office, he decided to move his firm into a brand new, sparkling office building. Since there was a severe shortage of office space at the time (as there usually is, every few years or so), my friend, Chuck, decided to rent nearly twice as much space as he needed at the moment for his firm. He then sublet the space he didn't need, earning a nice profit on other people's property (OPP).

Today smart real estate wealth builders are renting entire buildings and then subleasing them, or portions of them, to large firms. There are a number of advantages to you if you use such a plan, including:

1. No large down payment required
2. No title search, transfer tax, or other similar fees or expenses
3. Quicker (usually) takeover of the building
4. All rent payments made by you are usually fully tax deductible
5. No need to sell the building when you want to close your business

Renting a building and then subleasing it to others is more of a *business* activity than a real estate investment. So you lose some of the inherent advantages of real estate since in rental property you rent to others there is:

1. *No* depreciation to help offset your rental income (except some minor writeoffs for improvements you may make to the inside of the building).
2. *No* appreciation in value of your land or building since you don't own either.
3. *No* chance to re-finance your mortgage to give you tax-free cash.

Even though rental real estate which you sublease to others *does* have these disadvantages, let's take a quick look at a typical deal to see how you might profit from it.

## Rental Sublease Deal

You rent an 8-story office building containing 10,000 sq. ft. of floor area per floor for $7 per sq. ft. per year. Then you rent out various floors at the best rates you can get. Here's how your building rental expense and sublease income might work out.

*Rental Expenses:*

| | |
|---|---|
| Building rental cost to you per year = | |
|     8 stories x 10,000 sq.ft./story x $7/sq.ft. | = $560,000 |
| Building operating expenses (electricity, | |
|     labor, maintenance, insurance, etc.) | =   150,000 |
| Total annual cost to you | = $710,000 |

*Rental Income Per Year:*

| | |
|---|---|
| 10,000 sq.ft @ $8/sq.ft. | = $  80,000 |
| 30,000 sq.ft. @ $9/sq.ft. | =   270,000 |
| 20,000 sq.ft. @ $12/sq.ft. | =   240,000 |
| 20,000 sq.ft. @ $14/sq.ft. | =   280,000 |
| | |
| Total income | = $870,000 |
| Total annual cost | =   710,000 |
| Net income to you | = $160,000 |

So, by taking on a big building—such as this—with no cash down, you develop an income of about $160,000 per year. I say "about" because you might have other, unexpected expenses, which could reduce your income somewhat. However, I think you now see clearly the method, namely:

> You can make money from rented buildings with no cash down if you can rent out the space at a higher rate than you pay for the space.

*Note:* If you're wondering why the rental rates vary from one floor to another in the above example, it's because the rent *charged* varies with the:

1. Height above the ground
2. View offered by higher floors
3. Services the tenant gets with the rent

So the variations in the rent payment per square foot reflect these differences.

### PROFIT WHILE YOU CAN

"But," you ask, "why doesn't the owner rent out the building and make this income, instead of letting me do this?" There are any number of reasons why the owner might rather rent his entire building to one person, instead of many, including:

1. Only one tenant to deal with instead of many
2. Fewer leases, tenant credit checks, etc.
3. No maintenance headaches
4. Fewer vacancy problems

Some building owners would prefer to sun themselves in California or Florida while holding only one lease per building than to have the headaches that might come from 50 leases on space in the same building. Such owners are people who've "made it" in life. They have either earned enough for themselves or inherited enough to allow them to live without a struggle.

You can help such people (and there are more around than you might think) while earning big money for yourself by:

1. Running their buildings
2. Providing rental space for others
3. Earning a profit for the owner

To find buildings you can rent out profitably, look at the real estate columns of any large-city newspaper under these as well as other headings:

- Buildings for rent (commercial and residential)
- Buildings for sale (commercial and residential)
- Real estate opportunities

And keep in mind one key fact about rental buildings of all types, namely:

Renting a building can be your fastest and lowest-cost way to get into real estate without the need for a large cash outlay by yourself.

Think about this for a moment. Rental real estate could put one million dollars into your pocket in three years! And you do *NOT* need a big bundle of money to get started—less than $100 is often enough! And if you include an option to buy the building as part of your lease, you may eventually own it!

## COMBINE THE STOCK MARKET AND REAL ESTATE

You can start—with few investors—a real estate investment trust—REIT for short. Once your REIT is formed you can with proper legal guidance—sell shares of your REIT to the general public. Some REITs sell $10-million worth of shares before they own a square inch of land or one brick or one nail in a building! Others have sold as much as $50-million in shares *before* doing any business.

Your REIT can, if you wish, specialize in certain aspects of real estate, such as:

- Mortgages (short- or long-term)
- Construction funds (for 2-3 years)
- Real estate operation
- Second, or junior, mortgages
- Land and site development

Or if you wish—your REIT can go into any or all of these real estate activities. The big point to keep in mind is that:

> In a REIT you combine the magic power of OPM—Other People's Money—with the rapid growth of real estate and the potential rise in the value of the REIT shares on the stock market.

One beauty of selling shares in your REIT is that the equity money you receive for the shares is *not* a loan. Hence, you do *not* have to repay this money. Instead, you work hard to make the money grow in value as the real estate you control rises in value. REITs are discussed elsewhere in this book. I've covered them briefly again in this chapter because they are a unique example of how you can combine real estate with another business—in this case the stock market.

## MAKE THEATERS YOUR FORTUNE SOURCE

Theaters—as you know—require space—be they movie houses, legitimate theaters, outdoor movies, mini theaters, twin theaters, etc. Many a family—a few of whom I know—have lived, and are living—comfortable, easy-hour, no-stress lives on the income from theaters. And they get to see the latest shows free in their own theaters and in the theaters of their friends!

As a theater property owner or renter, you can:

1. Operate your theater on the property
2. Rent the property to a theater operator
3. Combine the theater with another business

For example, a theater owner I know of, runs his outdoor movie theater as a theater at night. But during the day he rents out his theater as a parking lot for commuters who don't want to drive all the way into the city. This owner got a local bus company to stop its buses at his lot to pick up passengers who parked their cars in his lot during the day!

And if you're artistically inclined—or your spouse is—you can run any kind of shows in your theater which appeal to you. If your choice matches the interests of the public, then you'll profit while enjoying the shows free! Also, your real estate holdings in the theater will probably be rising in value at the same time.

### OTHER REAL ESTATE-BASED BUSINESSES FOR YOU

There are many other real estate-based businesses which could pay you big profits while your real estate rises in value. These businesses include:

- Health clubs, gyms, etc.
- Bowling alleys, billiard parlors
- Golf courses, country clubs
- Motels, hotels, ranches
- Farms, citrus groves, timber lands
- Marinas, fishing stations, hunting lodges
- Ski slopes, ski lodges
- Theme parks, trailer parks
- Indoor tennis, outdoor tennis
- Plus many others

Often, people will invest in one or more of these businesses because they are more interested in immediate cash flow than in the long-term rise in real estate values. Yet—over a period of years—their real estate may pay them a larger return than their daily cash flow!

### TRY "MOVING REAL ESTATE" TO BUILD YOUR WEALTH

All real estate—no matter where it is located—has one common characteristic. This is the fact that:

Real estate is permanent—it does not move from one spot to another. The land remains where it was staked out on the deed.

Yet real estate often provides a number of common services, such as:

- Shelter from the elements
- Comfort, cover, convenience
- Status, location, enclosure

Certain "movable real estate" offers some of these services. The movable real estate I'm talking about includes:

- Boats, such as sailboats, house-boats, yachts, etc.
- Mobile homes, house trailers, campers
- Some luxury airplanes

Now, almost all movable real estate has certain characteristics, namely:

1. Movable real estate tends to go down in value with the passage of time
2. Movable real estate might be rented only part of any year
3. Movable real estate may require a relatively large labor force
4. Movable real estate may have large insurance costs

Yet I know plenty of people who own movable real estate who:

- Earn profits *every* year
- Get *big* depreciation tax deductions
- Enjoy their movable real estate regularly

Take Tim, who owns three boats which he rents out an average of 15 weeks a year. His average rental fee is $1,000 per week for a bare-boat charter (that is, without a paid captain). Such a charter is one in which the person who rents a boat for a period of time brings along the:

- Needed food
- Bedsheets, tablecloths, etc.
- Charts, navigation books
- Other necessities for cruising

So these items need not be supplied by Tim.

Tim's income averages $15,000 per year per boat. Since each boat cost about $50,000, Tim is able to deduct some $5,000 per year in depreciation (assuming a 10-year life for the boat). This means that the first $5,000 of income is completely tax free, for each boat. So Tim has a total of $15,000 a year in income which is free of any Federal, city or state income taxes.

Other legitimate tax deductions shelter more of this income. And since Tim is also a boating enthusiast besides being a businessman, he enjoys having three boats at his disposal any time he needs one.

And—like myself—Tim is a sun enthusiast. So he keeps two of his boats in Florida and one in the Caribbean during the winter. Any trips south he has to make during the winter from his home in the north to inspect or maintain his business properties are completely tax deductible, he says. "These expenses," Tim explains, "are ordinary and necessary for my business."

## GET OTHERS TO PAY FOR YOUR MOVABLE REAL ESTATE

I've done much thinking about and study of actual movable real estate deals. While you can own boats, mobile homes, campers, etc., as Tim does, your expenses *can* be high. The best way to own such "real estate" is through a limited partnership. This way you:

- Reduce, or eliminate, *your* investment
- Can buy more income producers (boats, campers, mobile homes, etc.)
- Spread the risk amongst many people
- Have greater ease in proving your business intentions

Yes, you *can* make money with movable real estate. One of the most successful gas station operators I know is a guy who owns a motor home and several campers, along with a slew of trailers, trucks, etc. His income from these often equals or exceeds the income from his gas and repair sales! And he's not fully dependent upon the sale of gas, oil, or repairs. This gives him more independence than he might otherwise have.

## MAKE YOUR FORTUNE IN REAL ESTATE-BASED BUSINESSES

You *can* make a quick, easy fortune from real estate-based businesses. In this chapter we've been able to mention only a few you can try. There are hundreds of other such businesses.

So resolve *today* to find yourself such a business. Then—when you make your fortune—drop me a note telling me how you did it. (I have a great publisher who forwards *all* my mail). I'll include your method in a future book to help other BWBs. (But to keep your success a secret, your name will *not* be used in the writeup). Now, go out and combine another business with real estate!

### Points to Remember

- You can often get 100% financing for a business other than real estate when you tie it in with real estate.
- Many businesses eventually earn more from their real estate investments than from their regular profit-making activities.
- There are seven easy steps to take to combine another business with real estate.
- Hundreds of different businesses can be "hinged" and leveraged around real estate.
- Real estate is a business, much like any other business.
- Always seek to obtain some income from your real estate even though you're more interested in another business.
- You can earn money by renting out rented property.
- You can usually make money from rented buildings with *no* cash down if you can rent out the space at a higher rate than you pay for it.
- To find buildings to rent out, look in the real estate columns of large city newspapers.
- Renting a building can be your fastest and lowest cost way to get into real estate without a large cash outlay.
- Other potentially profitable real estate related businesses include REITs, theaters, recreation facilities, motels, hotels, etc.
- "Movable real estate" might build your wealth while you enjoy it.

# 14

## HOW TO GO FROM PENNIES TO MILLIONS IN REAL ESTATE IN THREE YEARS, STARTING WITH NO CASH

This is the shortest chapter in this book because it gives you the 36 steps—one for each month—to go from pennies to millions in real estate in three years. Each month is numbered and you have a space for entering the date on which you complete a step. So start taking your first step now! Read the following steps carefully. Then, if you have any questions, refer to other parts of this book covering your question.

### FROM PENNIES TO MILLIONS IN REAL ESTATE IN THREE YEARS, STARTING WITH NO CASH

| Month No. | Check Off when Done | Your Action |
|---|---|---|
| 1 | _____ Date Done | Start building your real estate empire by reading this book from cover to cover and |

deciding which type of *income* real estate you'll use to build your fortune.

2 \
Date Done

Look for, and buy, your first income property using 100% financing. (Such a property will usually be priced at $35,000 to $50,000 and will require $5,000 in borrowed cash).

3 \
Date Done

Improve your first property by having it upgraded by making repairs, getting it fully rented, and making plans to raise the rents as soon as possible.

4 \
Date Done

Buy your second income property, using the upgraded value of No. 1 on your financial statement. Property No. 1 may now have a value of $50,000 to $65,000, based on the increased income and worth resulting from the improvements you made. Property No. 2 will probably be priced at $75,000 to $100,000 and will require $10,000 in borrowed cash.

5 \
Date Done

Devote this month to getting property No. 2 into shape so you can raise the rents and increase your cash income.

6 \
Date Done

Continue working on property No. 2 while you look for No. 3. Your No. 2 property will now probably have a value of $100,000 to $125,000. This value will look good on your financial statement.

7 \
Date Done

Locate property No. 3 and make an offer for it. This property will probably have a price of $200,000 to $250,000 and will require $25,000 in cash which you will borrow using the equity you have in properties No. 1 and No. 2.

8 \
Date Done

Buy property No. 3 using borrowed cash.

9 \
Date Done

Improve property No. 3 by making repairs, raising rents, etc.

10 \
Date Done

Continue working on all your properties.

11      _____      Survey your income and cash situation.
        Date Done       Make a summary of your net worth.
                        Thus:

|        | Property No. | Present Worth |
|--------|--------------|---------------|
|        | 1            | $ 65,000      |
|        | 2            | 125,000       |
|        | 3            | 275,000       |
| Total  |              | $465,000      |

12      _____      Take a month's vacation so you can enjoy
        Date Done  .    your new-found income!

13      _____      Look for property No. 4, which will have
        Date Done       a value of $300,000 to $400,000. Spend
                        at least four weeks looking for this prop-
                        erty because it will put you very close to
                        the millionaire class! If you need more
                        time to find your property, take it.

14      _____      Take over your property No. 4 during
        Date Done       this month. Use the increased value of
                        your first three properties to come up
                        with a "beautiful" financial statement.

15      _____      Improve property No. 4, if necessary.
        Date Done       Often, a property of this price will not
                        need much improvement because it is in
                        excellent condition at the start.

16      _____      Look for property No. 5. It will be in the
        Date Done       $350,000 price range. Again, use your
                        excellent financial statement as the basis
                        for borrowing *all* the cash you need.

17      _____      Take over property No. 5. You are now a
        Date Done       real estate millionaire, based on your five
                        properties. Thus:

| Property No. | Present Worth |
|--------------|---------------|
| 1            | $ 65,000      |
| 2            | 125,000       |
| 3            | 275,000       |

|   |   |
|---|---|
| 4 | 350,000 |
| 5 | 350,000 |

Total $1,165.000

Your MIF (=Money In Fist) income should be at least $100,000 a year.

18 _____
Date Done

Take a vacation to enjoy your wealth.

19-36 _____
Date Done

Here are 18 more months for you to work to get the money you seek, just in case:

(a) You're slower than others
(b) You have trouble finding suitable property
(c) Money tightens up
(d) Your wife or husband objects
(e) Etc.!

Even so, you can see how easy it is for *you* to make a million dollars in real estate in three years, starting with no cash!

### Points to Remember

• You *can* make a million in real estate in three years starting with *no* cash.
• The steps in this chapter are the keys to *your* wealth.

# HOW AND WHERE TO GET
# MORE DATA ON REAL ESTATE

"Knowledge is power,"—power to build *your* wealth faster, with fewer problems, and more surely. So here I'd like to give you many sources of more data on real estate. Why? Because by building your knowledge you will almost certainly build your wealth, for, as Aldous Huxley wrote:

> Every man who knows how to read has it in his power to magnify himself, to multiply the ways in which he exists, to make his life full, significant, and interesting.

Here are a number of sources of real estate data I'm certain you'll find helpful and profitable. Start using them today.

Available from Prentice-Hall, Inc., Englewood Cliffs, NJ 07632:

This firm is probably the largest publisher of real estate books and guides in the United States, if not the world. Their books and publications range from the beginner's how-to books to advanced works for professionals dealing in real estate. Here's a list of P-H books you'll find useful in building your real estate fortune. The price given is that at the time of publication of this book.

## REAL ESTATE INVESTMENT

Beaton, W.R., *Real Estate Investment,* 1971, $11.50.

Benke, W., *Land Investor's Profit Guide Negotiating Manual,* 1973, $19.95.

Bitney, F.L., *How to Buy Recreational Land for Profit,* 1970, $19.95.

Bockl, G., *How Real Estate Fortunes are Made,* 1972, $8.95.

Burleigh, D.R., *Double Your Money in Six Years: How to Reap Profits in Discounted Mortages, 1971, $8.95.*

ERC Editorial Staff, *Real Estate Man's Tax Desk Manual,* $34.95.

Kent, Robert, *How To Get Rich in Real Estate,* 1969, $8.95.

McMichael, S.L., *How to Make Money in Real Estate,* 1968, $8.95.

Mair, G., *Guide to Successful Real Estate Investing,* 1971, $12.95.

Nicely, G., *How to Reap Riches from Raw Land: Guide to Profitable Real Estate Speculation,* 1974, $8.95.

Peckham, J., *Master Guide to Income Property Brokerage,* 1968, $39.95.

Schraub, E., *Real Estate Investment Course,* 1968, $29.95.

Steinberg, J., *Mortgage Your Way to Wealth,* 1970, $8.95.

Lampley, J.B., *How to Go From Rags to Riches Fast with Sound Real Estate Investments,* 1975, $7.95.

## REAL ESTATE BUSINESS

Allen, J.B., *Selling Income Property Successfully,* 1970, $8.95.

Arnold, R.H., *How to Estimate Market Value in Selling Real Estate,* 1962, $8.95.

Barr, L. *Miracle Real Estate Guide,* 1965, $29.95.

Barrows, S., *Making Big Money in Real Estate,* 1967, $8.95.

Berman, D., *Urban Renewal: The Bonanza of the Real Estate Business,* 1969, $19.95.

Davey, H., *National Guide to Real Estate,* 1971, $10.50.

ERC Editorial Staff, *Today's Great Opportunities for Getting Rich in Real Estate,* 1974, $39.95.

Fass, G., *Fass System for Profits in Residential Income Property,* 1965, $16.95.

Gray, C., *Real Estate Sales Contracts,* 1973, $22.95.

Gross, J., *Illustrated Encyclopedic Dictionary of Real Estate Terms,* 1969, $16.00.

Hussander, M., *How to Use Syndicates to Make Money in Local Real Estate,* 1973, $22.95.

Mair, G., *Guide to Successful Real Estate Investing, Buying, Financing and Leasing,* 1971, $12.95.

Moser, L., *How to Build a Fortune in Real Estate,* 1965, $8.95.

P-H Editorial Staff, *Real Estate Guide,* 1966, $45.00.
Riffel, M., *How to Combine Wild Imagination with Creative Thinking to Make Big Money in Real Estate,* 1973, $34.95.
Smith, G., *Master Guide to Real Estate Valuation,* 1973, $49.95.

Available from International Wealth Success, Inc., Bank Plaza, Merrick, NY 11566:

*Real Estate Riches Fortune Building Course.* $99.50. Contains 7 useful guides showing you how to make $1-million, or more, in real estate as an income-property owner, mortgage banker, mortgage broker, property developer, etc. Gives you the data you need to get started in quick *speed-read* form. This big Course has helped many BWBS get started.

*Fast Financing of Real Estate Wealth Course.* $99.50. Gives numerous ways to get money for real estate, including modern borrowing methods, equity (stock) capital, syndications, etc. Covers many types of income real estate. This big Course, which features *speed-read* information, could get *you* the real estate money you need.

*Financial Broker/Finder/Business Broker/Consultant Course.* $99.50. A *speed-read* course that shows you how to get started as a financial broker earning fees for finding money for others, working as a finder to earn fees in a variety of ways, or the earning of fees as a business broker or consultant. This big Course also includes four diploma-like membership certificates which you can mount on your office walls.

*Business Borrowers Complete Success Kit.* $99.50. Shows both beginning and experienced wealth builders how, and where, they can borrow money for real estate and business use. Gives many practice forms the BWB can use. Includes hundreds of sources of loans for real estate and business.

*Zero-Cash Success Techniques for Building Great Wealth.* $99.50. Shows how to get started making $1-million, beginning with no cash, in real estate or in business. Covers many different zero-cash methods which could help you build your fortune. Includes a 58-minute tape on small business financing by Ty Hicks.

*Raising Money from Grants and Other Sources.* $99.50. This big Course shows you how to raise money that never has to be repaid, if you do the work for which the Grant was made. Gives the information you need to start getting grants for real estate from foundations, the Federal, state, or city government, or from large corporations. Also covers fund raising.

*Mail-Order/Direct-Mail Riches Course.* $99.50. The professional approach to building your riches in mail-order/direct-mail in the fastest way possible. This big Course will help you save money in all mail-order/direct-mail activities in real estate and any other business in which you might use these ways of selling your products.

*Franchise Riches Course.* $99.50. Thought to be the only course of its kind, this big program shows you how to collect fees from your business ideas which help people make money. So, instead of you paying others to use their business ideas, people pay to use your ideas. Typical franchise fees can range from $500 to $50,000, or more.

*The Radical New Road to Wealth,* by A. David Silver. $15.00. Comprehensive discussion of venture capital by a young venture capitalist who has helped raise more than $30-million. Tells you what you need to do to get the venture capital you seek for real estate or any other business.

*60-Day Fully Financed Fortune Course.* $29.50. Shows you how to start and run a funding company in which you borrow money which you lend out at a profit. Gives you step-by-step and day-by-day how-to tips which can get *you* started in 60 days, or less.

*Starting Millionaire Success Course.* $99.50. This is a big Course covering real estate, mail order, export-import and other businesses which you can start or take over to begin earning your first million in business. Features *speed-read* lessons which are interesting and practical. This course could be just what *you* need to get going—now.

# INDEX